CREATING THE
ACCOUNTABLE
ORGANIZATION

MARK SAMUEL

CREATING THE
ACCOUNTABLE
ORGANIZATION

A PRACTICAL
GUIDE TO
PERFORMANCE
EXECUTION

XEPHOR
PRESS

© 2006 Mark Samuel

XEPHOR
P R E S S

Xephor Press
3 Holly Hill Lane
Katonah, NY 10536
www.xephorpress.com
1-914-232-6708

ISBN 0-9752638-5-4

Printed and bound in the United States of America.

CONTENTS

PART TWO

INTRODUCTION:

Achieve Breakthrough Results

CREATING AN ACCOUNTABLE ORGANIZATION IS THE SUBJECT OF THIS BOOK. Developing a culture where "people at all levels of the organization can be *counted on* to keep their commitments and agreements" is our focus. Unlike other books on accountability, you will learn strategies and techniques for increasing both *individual* and *shared* accountability. This includes within and between teams as well as between different departments.

This book is for leaders and change agents at any level within an organization who are ready to move to the next level of excellence and success. If you or your organization is stuck where you are and are ready to get unstuck, this book is for you. If you are part of a benchmark organization and are looking for ways to ensure that you remain a benchmark in three years, this book is for you. If the performance in your organization has flattened and you want to lead it to its next level, this book is for you. If you have read other books on management or accountability and still found that something was missing, then this book is for you. This book is aimed at challenging preconceived notions of leadership and accountability. Every concept in this book is based on practical experience instead of theoretical models—more than twenty years of implementing change, research, and learning from our mistakes as well as our successes.

Increasing accountability improves performance and morale. We've seen it happen:

- A hospital's cross-functional middle management team reduced operating costs by $4.3 million within three months exceeding its cost reduction goal of $3.9 million.

- A longstanding high-tech company doubled the number of projects sold, increased market share, and reduced operating costs within twelve months.

- A retail chain increased productivity by 30 percent, increased sales commissions by 20 percent (breaking previous records), and improved customer and employee satisfaction within six months.

- A utility company reduced control room deficiencies and corrective maintenance backlog by 25 percent and reduced safety-related corrective actions from 900 to less than 115 (breaking organizational records) in less than six months.

- A hospital increased average patient satisfaction 25 percent within nine months.

- An international petroleum company achieved its productivity goals for the first time in five years while improving morale by 25 percent.

Creating an Accountable Organization shows how to lead your business so it remains effective, competitive, and successful in the face of continual pressure to perform at higher levels. This book gives you practical strategies and tools used by leading organizations in diverse industries to achieve breakthrough results. Although continuous improvement is important, the speed at which organizations can make dramatic changes and paradigm shifts determines their positions in a global competitive market. As Jack Welch is quoted in the book, *Jack Welch Speaks*, by Janet Lowe, "Speed is everything . . . Speed keeps businesses and people young."[1]

1. Janet Lowe, *Jack Welch Speaks: Wisdom from the World's Greatest Business Leader*, John Wiley & Sons, Inc., 1998.

We have come to rely on strategic planning and goal setting, only to find that we are adding more and more priorities to our plates before we are accomplishing our old ones. We thought that the focus on competencies would solve the problem, but we found that competencies are changing as fast as the new business environment, so we still can't keep up. We are going from one flavor-of-the-week change to another and spending more time on activities that produce change, but they aren't providing bottom-line enhancements and business results.

The increase of organizational accountability that results in improved morale, trust, and performance stems from:

- Transforming meaningless activities (including ineffective meetings, overused task forces, and never-ending restructuring) into meaningful actions, where decisions are made that move the organization forward

- Improving performance execution in addition to streamlining processes

- Having the courage to address nonperformers who survive at the expense of hard-working top performers

High Performance Requires Accountability

Performance execution represents the link between people necessary for achieving desired outcomes. This involves coordinating tasks and projects, making decisions, sharing resources, and implementing change. An organization can have streamlined processes and skilled employees and still not achieve its goals if its employees aren't executing effectively. It's during performance execution that accountability is in tact or breaks down.

When there is a lack of accountability, people don't get information when they need it, decisions aren't made when action is required, and people don't receive guidance or support when faced with new challenges.

When there is a lack of accountability, nonperformers thrive while the rest of us do double work picking up the slack. When there is a lack of accountability, communication breaks down, territorialism increases, and recognition for success disappears. When there is a lack of accountability, people often fall into a victim mode of fighting each other, rebelling against change, and protecting themselves at the cost of hurting others and the company.

People are stressed by the effort needed to keep up with endless changes being made in organizations. But more important, they are burned out by the lack of accountability in the workplace where they have to work twice as hard to make up for those who aren't accountable. This nightmare has to stop, for the sake of all employees and the survival of our businesses.

Accountability Is a Bigger Issue Than We Thought

Over the past three years, we have surveyed more than 1,100 people from fifteen different industries, across all levels of organization. When we developed our "Organizational Accountability Assessment," we expected that most organizations would score between 70 and 85 out of a possible score of 100. However, the average accountability index turned out to be only 57 out of a possible score of 100, and with no significant difference in overall scores between management and nonmanagement.

Problem #1: Overwhelming and competing priorities. Of all of the questions on the survey, the one that had the lowest score involved clear and aligned direction. People at all levels responded that their organization was fragmented with overwhelming and competing priorities. *This breaks a critical foundation of accountability.* To be accountable, you must clearly know your desired outcomes—what you are accountable for achieving. Without that clarity, accountability cannot exist.

Problem #2: Territorialism and silos. The next lowest scores involved the issues of cross-functional team leadership and taking ownership for solving problems. Again, people at all levels felt that their organizations were riddled with territorialism and silos in an environment of blame and finger-pointing. No matter how effective your processes and abilities are within your organization, if you aren't effectively *coordinating* projects and activities due to silos and territorialism, and if you move into blame and finger-pointing when a problem surfaces, there is no way you can execute effectively to achieve successful business results.

Problem #3: Avoidance. To make matters worse, the next lowest score involved problem and conflict avoidance, meaning that when people weren't blaming each other for problems, they were avoiding them completely.

You can complete the free Organizational Accountability Assessment to assess your organization's accountability index by going to our Web site at www.impaqcorp.com.

Characteristics of an Accountable Organization

The word *accountability* usually conjures up pictures of a room full of people, all ducking behind their chairs and pointing their fingers at someone else, shouting, "It's their fault!" *This has nothing to do with being accountable.* In fact, if you are using accountability in response to a mistake or problem, it is too late! What's more, people who use accountability as a way to blame others are only hiding in a "victim" mode and avoiding their own involvement.

In an accountable organization, people ask for support when it is needed, rather than waiting until there is a crisis that causes a major breakdown. People don't just take responsibility for the problems in their area; instead, they look for ways to support improved performance in the areas they impact outside of their direct job description.

Accountability is the basis for having an environment of trust, support, and dedication to excellence. With accountability, people can depend on each other and don't have to worry about doing extra work because others failed to keep their agreements. When people are keeping their commitments and agreements, frustration and stress go down, while teamwork goes up. In an environment where it is safe to address issues that lead to bettering the organization, conflicts and differences are allowed to surface, where they can be resolved, rather than forcing them underground, where they fester.

When people are accountable to each other, the resulting synergy creates new solutions that no one person could have developed. When people are accountable, they implement good solutions effectively. Many times, they accomplish their results in half the time expected, because of the participation and commitment of everyone as a team. When there is accountability, people feel supported during the most difficult times, whether it is dealing with a work-related situation or a personal challenge that, even peripherally, affects their work. If you want to find an example of an accountable organization, look for any winning basketball team, dance company, symphony orchestra, or any organization that is exceeding expectations against all odds. Accountability is power!

Your Personal Road to Success

I was taught that information is power. Even today, I hear about people who hoard information as a way of gaining influence. However, one of my mentors, Charlie Brotman, shared with me these words of advice: "If you want to rise in your career within any organization, having information is important, but it doesn't give you power unless you do something with it. If you want to gain influence, you must be accountable. If people can depend on you for results, they will come to you when they need help. They will come to you when they need support because they will gain confidence in you based on your results. They will ask you for information, even if they know you don't have it, because they know you will get the information in a timely manner. When you are accountable, people can trust you because you keep your word. And when you can't, you are up-front with them. Be accountable, and you will automatically be successful!"

Can you imagine promoting anyone who is not accountable? Accountability is clearly the single most important characteristic for increasing someone's responsibilities in the workplace: you must be able to count on them for getting results. In fact, your top performers are inevitably those whom you can count on to achieve their business goals while supporting other team members. Whether you are developing managers to be better leaders and coaches, or you are developing employees to improve customer service and critical thinking, you must instill accountability to transform learning into performance and performance into results. Accountability is the primary value for promoting individuals into positions of leadership and greater responsibility. And, accountability equates to job security.

Accountability Is Not an Option; It's a Necessity

Some say that accountability is the next fad, the next flavor-of-the-month change. However, accountability (or the lack of accountability) has been with us all of our lives and throughout history. It isn't going away because you don't like it, because it is difficult, or because you think there is a better way. Ultimately, nothing gets accomplished and change doesn't happen if you aren't accountable. It is always present. We either have the choice of increasing our accountability or operating from a mode of ignoring problems and blaming others when things go wrong. Accountability is a necessity for any person, team, or organization that is determined to be successful and to sustain their success.

Organizations that have developed systems of accountability have achieved sustainable results. Some have become benchmarks in their industries for more than ten years. Others have made short-term improvements and then learned to sustain those improvements for many years. It is one thing to set and achieve a goal. It is another thing to sustain that achievement and continue to improve through different leaders, through mergers, and through other changes that would otherwise sabotage success.

Ten Deadly Sins that Prevent Us from Achieving Results

Sin #1: Overassessment. We're guilty of committing this sin when too much assessment of a problem is completed, either to determine needs for change or to analyze a new process, technology, or system before it is implemented. Overassessment results in paralysis and lost opportunity. For example, a community college is planning to make fundamental changes to increase enrollment in its classes. This is critical, because state funding is being slashed and the college's customer base is shrinking. It has been talking about this goal for two years, and even with board approval, it's still not moving forward. The college is busy analyzing the changes, discussing them, and defending the need to make them, although some don't like it. The only thing the college isn't doing is taking action to improve the situation. At the same time, other colleges in the area are creating partnerships in the community to increase their enrollments.

Sin #2: Plan to perfection. We're guilty of committing this sin when we want our plan to be perfect in hopes that we can make the "nay-sayers" comfortable and prevent their criticism. We also hope that a perfect plan will lead to perfect implementation to prevent the typical chaos that occurs. In trying to ensure that everyone remains comfortable by being involved in the change, we end up fostering conflict and confusion that leads to even greater resistance. By the time the plan is implemented, our lack of responsiveness during the planning process increases the pressure to achieve results. There is nothing like a perfect plan to create resistance from those implementing the plan who will get blamed if something goes wrong during implementation.

Sin #3: Communicate for buy-in. We're guilty of this sin when we are so invested in people feeling comfortable with our plans that we take months to communicate it. We make our presentation, nice and pretty, selling the program to ensure that everyone will like it. Then, when people resist in spite of our sales pitch, we either change our message to appease them, causing a lack of credibility, or we commit Sin #1 once again by conducting yet another reassessment, which delays implementation even further. When you "sell" your plan for change, you create a negative reaction from those who know "that there is a downside" and wonder why you are avoiding that in your presentation.

Sin #4: Empower instead of guide. We're guilty of this sin when we create a wonderful plan for change, but then we empower others to implement the plan, thereby abdicating our own involvement as managers or leaders. Some managers don't even bother to prepare their direct reports for implementation. They are generally the same managers who punish their people when they fail, but they never make any attempt to coach people to success. Other managers empower employees after the plan is complete. Unfortunately, we are better at planning a strategy than we are at planning its execution. This leaves employees feeling abandoned and directionless, resulting in even greater confusion and conflict.

Sin #5: Avoid monitoring progress. We are guilty of this sin when we avoid monitoring our progress in order to avoid facing "bad news." If we don't monitor, we avoid the risk of discovering we aren't on track to be successful. Also, if we don't monitor our team or staff, then we don't have to coach them if the results are off-track. Without monitoring and measuring progress, we can avoid conflict, problems, and the need to admit to upper management that we are not reaching our goals. However, by not monitoring progress, we may stray even further off-track without knowing it and diminish the likelihood of recovery.

Sin #6: Expect perfection. We are guilty of this sin when we believe that we have the perfect plan, that we have communicated the plan perfectly, and now we expect perfect implementation and execution. If everyone keeps all their commitments and agreements, we will have perfect success. Right? Wrong. Human beings aren't perfect, and mistakes will be made. For example, Larry Brown, coach of the Detroit Pistons—the 2004 NBA Champions—said it well in an interview in *USA Today:* "Our game is a game of mistakes. I tell our players that if you're not making mistakes, you're not trying to win. I don't mean mistakes from lack of effort. But I don't want anyone to fear losing. I want them to fear not giving their best effort."[2]

Sin #7: Measuring business outcomes without measuring performance execution. We are guilty of this sin when we use measurable indicators to inspire improved performance without linking them to performance execution, which only causes people to work harder at what is not working to get those results. To increase accountability for performance, managers are using performance indicators related to customer satisfaction, productivity, quality, operating costs, and profitability. These are important for knowing where the business stands in terms of its business health, just as an athletic team would measure wins and losses.

This would be like a basketball coach saying we have to win more games, but not assisting the team in changing their habits of defense to limit opponents' scoring or improving the offense so they achieve more points during each game. Ultimately, the way to achieve better business results is through improved processes and performance execution.

Sin #8: Avoid holding people accountable. We are guilty of this sin when we establish no consequences for those who are sabotaging the success of the team and the organization. This is rooted in our desire to be nice, to give everyone a chance to be heard, and to make everyone comfortable. Certainly, the prospect of overwhelming new responsibilities may cause anyone to resist even the most positive changes. It may be appropriate, even constructive, to resist a change when it is first discussed or implemented. This is when a devil's advocate position may still be helpful. However, when someone resists a change well after it

2. *USA Today*, Section B, Talking Business with Ron Insana, February 21, 2005.

has been implemented and the new norms have been established, it undermines the success and demoralizes those who are trying to make it work. We have all witnessed failure after initial success due to a group of negativists who never gave the change a chance to work. They are actually empowered to sabotage because there are no penalties to discourage them.

Sin #9: Fostering the "Blame Game." We are guilty of this sin when we tend to blame other departments, corporate office, or management when problems occur rather than addressing those that aren't performing effectively in our own department. We allow our disappointment or embarrassments for not performing perfectly to get the best of us and cause us to attack others for mistakes or low performance. Instead of focusing on learning and identifying the process or aspect of performance execution that needs improvement, we put the responsibility on anyone else to protect ourselves from looking bad. Blame creates more blame, resulting in an environment of fear and mediocrity.

Sin #10: Fail to recognize success. We are guilty of this sin when we can't even determine whether the plan was successful; we haven't monitored our progress so we have no way of recognizing success. Without such performance data, we can't possibly acknowledge people for their contributions. So we don't. We speed on to the next program, leaving people frustrated, with no sense of completion or acknowledgment for their hard work. As a result, we not only have a failed effort, we have demoralized employees.

Anatomy of Accountability and Achieving Breakthrough Results

There are eight elements consistently present in accountable organizations:

1. Clear Vision and Priorities. Accountable organizations know exactly where they are going and what they are going to accomplish. This isn't a goal statement, but a clear picture of success stated as a result. This includes the desired outcome and the desired culture. Accountable organizations not only have a clear vision, but also a clear set of priorities that all leaders know and are aligned to accomplish.

2. Shared Ownership. In most organizations, each executive is only responsible for the priorities assigned to him or her. In an accountable organization, each executive has a shared accountability for all of the top priorities. Although they may not lead the priority project, they are accountable for monitoring progress, participating in the solving of problems associated with each priority, and sharing resources to achieve priority results. This is demonstrated through interdependence and integrating people, processes, and skills to produce the stated results. An amazing synergy takes place when all parties step forward and produce at this level—everyone wins!

3. Effective Execution. Performance execution is the process of linking people and processes to achieve high performance. It is represented by the qualities of coordination, timing, communication, decision making, and actions necessary to achieve desired outcomes. Although it is often thought of as the "soft side" of performance, execution is practiced and rehearsed by the best professional performing groups—whether in the field of drama, music, sports, or dance. Ultimately, execution determines whether you succeed or fail in accomplishing your desired actions.

4. Relentless Attack of Dysfunctional Habits. We all have bad habits that keep us from accomplishing our goals. Generally, we maintain these habits to remain comfortable instead of enduring the struggle, discipline, and sometimes pain of correcting a bad situation. Sometimes it involves analysis paralysis, other times it involves ineffective meetings that waste people's time. Sometimes our habits are attempting to get consensus from everyone before we make a decision, whereas other times we don't include impacted departments when making decisions that impact them. Accountable leaders, however, make it a point to surface and address these and other dysfunctional habits. They develop new effective habits and establish measurements to ensure that effective habits are reinforced.

5. Surface and Resolve Problems and Conflicts. Whereas most organizations hide problems and keep unresolved conflicts underground, accountable organizations have the courage and the process to address issues. No one is afraid of being punished or fired. The focus is not on "whose fault it is," but on how the issue is going to get resolved. When conflicts are surfaced, people address them directly with the people involved and have a clear process for reaching resolution. No resentments. No retribution. Just an environment of trust, openness, and honest communication.

6. Proactive Recovery. Accountable organizations recognize that successful people make mistakes and, therefore, put recovery plans in place. You may fail to anticipate future challenges. Sometimes you don't keep commitments. When the unexpected happens, does your organization end up in crisis? Success is a matter of being prepared to handle inevitable glitches. Effective recovery requires that everyone involved be prepared to make corrections as they are needed during execution. When you demand perfection, you create a tension that almost always ensures screw-ups. When perfection is demanded, people cover up their errors, which go unresolved until they blow up into a major crisis. When excellence is the objective, people do their best and know that, instead of being *punished* for surfacing an obstacle, they will be *supported* in solving problems—a process that ultimately results in success.

> The focus is not on "whose fault it is," but on how the issue is going to get resolved.

7. Measuring Performance Execution. Measurement of results is used by most organizations to determine success or failure. However, by the time they measure results, it's too late: the results are in. Accountable organizations identify the key indicators for successful performance execution and identify measurements to ensure that those indicators are the focus. They measure key attributes of their culture that link to business results as well as performance.

8. Recognize Success. An organization can't be accountable for mistakes if it is not accountable for success. Measurement is not only used to focus on the effective habits that get results, but it also is used as a way to recognize successful results to ensure that people feel a sense of accomplishment. In an accountable organization, recognizing results is a daily activity shared by managers and nonmanagers alike. Everyone takes pride and acknowledges each other for successful results. Being part of a successful organization is what inspires people to put forth their best effort and to get great results.

An Accountability Case Study:
How One Telecommunications Company Succeeded at All Eight Elements

Accountability is important at every level of an organization. One of my favorite examples of team accountability involved a group of line workers at a leading telecom company. One of the team members described with great pride his team's impact on the organization. This team had its resources diminished when the organization was experiencing major cutbacks and eventual downsizing. Instead of becoming victim to the cuts, this team decided on its own (without intervention from myself or any other consultant) that it would rise above the cuts and increase the team's performance and productivity without additional resources. This is their story, told in terms of the process of accountability described earlier:

1. Clear Vision and Priorities. At one of their team meetings, a team member led the group to create an intention of becoming the best-functioning team in the organization during this crisis period. They observed the whining and complaining of others in the organization regarding the budget cuts, and they created the clear intention to remain positive, be supportive, and strive for high performance. They pictured their team as being highly effective, sharing resources, supporting one another to accomplish the desired outcomes, and conducting their own effort to improve processes and reduce costs. Ultimately, they saw themselves as a high-performing team where they recognized each other's successes, developed each other's skills, and distanced themselves from those outside the team who were more negative.

2. Shared Ownership. Before they left the meeting, they made sure that everyone on the team agreed to put the team's needs above their own individual needs. This didn't mean that they would ignore individual issues. In fact, if an individual had a problem, he or she would bring it up to the team for support, rather than remaining silent. They agreed to review their commitment once a month to make sure they were on track.

3. Effective Execution. They took it upon themselves to improve their coordination, communication, and productivity by reviewing their processes and the way in which they were performing their jobs. It turned out that their processes were fairly streamlined, but they were wasting resources by not sharing more and by not communicating their activities with each other. This was improved and costs were cut.

---

4. Relentless Attack of Dysfunctional Habits. Up to this point, the team didn't meet with each other to share best practices or make improvements. Through their new process of being a team, they developed a habit of meeting for the purpose of surfacing and resolving problems and discussing resolved challenges. Meetings were kept efficient and on purpose.

5. Surface and Resolve Problems and Conflicts. One of the team members began coming late to work. Rather than letting it become an issue with their supervisor, his teammates challenged him in a supportive but accountable manner at one of their meetings. As a result, a new agreement was created for showing up to work on time. This agreement was reviewed at the subsequent meetings. The problem was resolved.

6. Proactive Recovery. After about nine months, the equipment they were using broke down during the night shift. Because they had a recovery process in place, they were able to get other team members to come in to work to assist with the clean up and resolve the breakdown. Also, they immediately held an emergency meeting to discuss alternatives for replacing equipment in a more proactive manner.

7. Measuring Performance Execution. They tracked their responsiveness to solving line problems and tracked a linear improvement in reaction time and response to breakdowns. At the end of the year, the team calculated cost reductions, better utilization of resources, and better customer service through response times.

8. Recognize Success. After the team measured results, they went out and celebrated their success. They didn't share with me much about their party. However, at the next meeting, they decided to write a report and share their results with upper management. About six months later, an executive attended one of their meetings. He congratulated the group for their effort and contributions as a team. Whereas the rest of the organization was continuing to experience budget cuts, the executive asked the team what additional changes could make their jobs even more effective. He said, "You successfully demonstrated that we can trust you to make the best of your situation and achieve meaningful results. Therefore, we want to support you in doing more of that in the future."

Accountable Leaders Are Heroes: How This Book Can Help You Become a Hero

When times are challenging and survival is in question, it is time for heroes. Who are those heroes? *You* can be. Heroes start out as ordinary people who see what is necessary and begin doing it, even if by current measure, it is considered extraordinary. *Creating an Accountable Organization* provides all you need to know to become a hero; to produce the results; to survive, prosper, and take your associates along with you.

The way is clear. It may not be easy, but you can do it. It requires making the tough decisions that keep organizations progressing. You must surface the problems that prevent success and facilitate solutions.

Part of the process is asking yourself whether everything you do or assign to others is *meaningful action* or just pointless activity. That means eliminating unproductive meetings and coaching nonperformers who are sabotaging success and morale. It requires developing skills to lead with a greater sense of urgency, a clearer strategy, a focus on performance execution, and a higher level of responsiveness.

In short, it involves being more accountable and creating more accountability within the work environment so employees experience being supported.

Part 1 of this book, "Break Away from Old Leadership Paradigms," challenges widely used leadership practices and reveals the breakdowns and victimization that results from these practices. It replaces the myths with "truths of leadership" that foster organization-wide accountability and catapult performance to new standards of excellence.

Part 2, "Six Strategies for Leading with Accountability," provides the essential systems and techniques for developing an accountable organization and leadership practices that produce incredible results.

Implementing these strategies will produce a highly spirited workforce that achieves more, does it faster, and experiences quality performance and desired, breakthrough results that are sustained over time. In this edition of the book, new processes are included and modifications to previous practices are provided based on learning from the successful organizations implementing accountability practices. And throughout the book, we've included lots of examples as well as detailed case studies (look for them in the shaded boxes).

Accountability is a process of continual improvement, and there is no panacea. However, we must have the courage to let go of those parts of our old paradigm that are no longer effective. We must have the courage to take risks, to continue on our path of self-improvement. It is time for bold action to make work life more meaningful and effective at getting results so that customers can be better served, organizations can be profitable, and employees can feel a sense of accomplishment and fulfillment. Let's get started!

GLOSSARY OF TERMS

Acknowledge—communicate directly with a person, sharing your perception of the situation in a caring, nonjudgmental manner.

Blind Survey—a second assessment where participants do not see their ratings or scores from the original assessment. This is a way to achieve less bias in rating or scores.

Comfort Zone—a state of feeling sufficiently satisfied with the current conditions of your job (or other aspects of your life) such that you wouldn't want to make a change.

Habits—behaviors automatically, consistently, and regularly demonstrated. Some habits are purposeful, and some are "the way we have always done things here."

Measurement—the means for tracking progress on improvement goals, changed habits, and business outcomes including tangible and intangible indicators.

Mind-set—beliefs, perceptions, and viewpoints about a situation.

Mission—a statement representing the purpose or charter of a team.

Organizational Accountability—a working environment where people take actions to keep performance-related commitments and communication-related agreements.

Performance Execution—the actions, interactions, behaviors, and communication necessary to achieve business outcomes. Performance execution implies linkage between people to achieve desired outcomes.

Personal Accountability—individual choice to take actions consistent with your desired outcomes.

Proactive Recovery—planned and agreed upon strategy for mobilizing resources or taking action to address a breakdown or unexpected.

Punishment Zone—a working condition in which a person could be punished for attempting to make a major change. This could include losing your job, getting demoted, or even being embarrassed in front of your colleagues in a team meeting.

Safety Zone—a state of perceived security allowing someone to take risks involved with change.

Shared Accountability—a working environment where individuals take ownership for the success of a project, team, or organization regardless of individual position.

Significant Improvement—this does not refer to "statistically significant," but to having an increase or decrease of 25 percent or more in a rating or score.

Success Factors (of Performance Execution)—new habits in the form of behaviors, actions, and attitude to replace old habits required to achieve the vision.

Support—clarify, renegotiate, or assist a person without doing his or her task for him or her.

Vision—a future picture of success (desired outcomes) representing a "stretch" or improvement that guides the development of new habits of performance execution.

PART ONE

BREAK AWAY FROM OLD LEADERSHIP PARADIGMS

Unleash Ability Through Accountability

Create an Accountable Culture: Stop Avoiding the Real Issues!

Three Traps of Ineffective Leadership

The Formula to Achieve Breakthroughs

Leadership Roles that Produce Breakthrough Results

CHAPTER 1

UNLEASH ABILITY
THROUGH
ACCOUNTABILITY

> **MYTH:** Accountability is a way to blame someone for making a mistake, resulting in fear.
>
> **TRUTH:** Accountability is the key for increasing trust, reducing fear, and improving morale and performance.

THE HUGELY SUCCESSFUL *DILBERT* COMIC STRIP clearly strikes a chord deep within the heart of the corporate world. Much of its humor arises from the low levels of accountability within Scott Adams' mythical corporation, where management trainees are instructed to "Never be in the same room as a decision." There, we encounter the Evil H.R. Director, who reminds the boss to be sure to avoid contact with subordinates. A quick tour of the *Dilbert* Web site produces this gem of corporate wisdom from the Center for Executive DUHcision-Making: "Informed decision making comes from a long tradition of guessing and then blaming others for inadequate results."

We laugh, but by exposing the painful "truths" of the corporate world, exaggerated though they may be, Scott Adams has started us off on the road to recovery. Because to laugh at our weaknesses means to acknowledge them. And once we have acknowledged their existence, we can begin to address them.

Personal accountability is a key driver for organizational accountability and is fully described in our book, *The Power of Personal Accountability*. However, organizational accountability goes beyond personal accountability. *Creating the Accountable Organization* offers a systematic approach to increasing organizational accountability, which encompasses all of the following:

- "Shared accountability" between leaders

- Team accountability

- Project accountability

- Personal accountability

Accountability Starts at the Top: A Case Study

A CEO of a medium-sized high-tech organization called me into his office and complained, "No one around here is accountable for anything. Everyone is busy, but no one is accountable!" I asked him what would be different if people were accountable. He responded, "Projects would get completed on time and within budget. If everyone would just take accountability and do their jobs, we would be successful."

Clearly, he viewed accountability as an all-or-nothing event. I asked, "If everyone was individually accountable and completed their own tasks but didn't coordinate their activities with project teammates, would projects get completed on time?"

"No," he replied. "We would have to establish processes for people to work together in a project team. Then, they would be fully accountable."

I further asked him, "If each project team completed its tasks by coordinating with each other, but didn't share information with other project teams and functional departments, would your organization still be successful?"

Looking a little discouraged, he responded, "No. We would have duplication of effort, wasted resources, and delayed or poor decisions. If we are to be fully accountable and successful, people must complete their own tasks, coordinate among teammates, and share information with other project teams and functional departments."

"So it sounds like accountability is more than people just doing their jobs?" I asked.

"Right," he agreed. "But if people aren't doing their own jobs, then the remaining parts of accountability can't happen."

I told him he was absolutely right, and I added that everyone needs clear expectations, guidance, and coaching in order to be successful and to be fully accountable. "So now," I said, "let's talk about how many people you have either coached or let go for nonperformance."

With a look of shock, he responded, "None. I guess accountability begins with me."

The Five Levels of Accountability

Accountability is an *evolutionary* process that can have a *revolutionary* impact on an organization. There are distinct levels of organizational accountability with predictable characteristics at each level. Figure 1-1 details the range of accountability, from "Entitlement" (no accountability) to "Organizational Accountability" (complete accountability).

Within your organization, you will find some managers and employees functioning at lower levels of accountability, and others

Figure 1-1: The Accountability Continuum

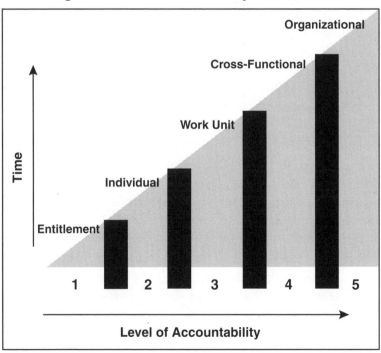

Figure 1-2:
Typical Accountability Levels in an Organization

Lower Organizational Accountability		Higher Organizational Accountability		
1	2	3	4	5

functioning at higher levels, so that if you were to chart the organization's level of accountability it would resemble a bell curve distribution.

Figure 1-2 illustrates the difference between two organizations, one with a lower level of accountability and the other with a higher level of accountability. Notice the people missing from each organization. The organization with lower accountability won't be able to retain highly accountable performers. The high performer will get frustrated by the lack of accountability and leave. An organization with a higher level of accountability will lose the lower performers because they won't be able to take the pressure of needing to be more accountable.

Let's look at each level of accountability in detail.

Level 1: Entitlement

One of my first jobs was working for a state hospital in California. I was given an assignment by the hospital administrator to gather information. I will never forget going to another department and asking for specific data I knew existed. The clerical administrator told me politely that she had the data I was seeking, and then returned to her work without retrieving it for me.

Surprised, I asked her if she was busy, or if there was some other problem. No, she wasn't really busy, and there was no problem. Then she picked up the phone and made a call to her sister. By this time, I was not only frustrated but also furious about the lack of responsiveness. I waited for seven minutes, and then in exasperation, I asked her if she would please get me the data I was requesting and explained the importance of the assignment to the hospital administrator. "No," she replied calmly. "It's not my job."

When an organization is plagued by an attitude of entitlement, employees are paid for showing up on the job regardless of performance.[1] There are no expectations for performance, and people are free to perform in any manner that is comfortable to them. Convenience determines effort. Ultimately, morale is low from the indifference that everyone has for his or her own performance and for each other's performance.

Level 2: Individual Accountability

Individual accountability is an improvement on entitlement. At this level, employees take responsibility for completing their own assignments based on their own job descriptions, without concern for the impact they may have on others. People are competitive with their teammates, and support is minimal. Consistency of performance across the organization is low, and fragmentation of work efforts and projects is high. This creates a high degree of frustration.

People have to work harder to improve their performance because they can depend only on themselves, in isolation from the rest of the team and organization. Coordination of effort is low, and resources are poorly utilized. Decisions are made without regard for the impact on teammates or others within the organization.

Level 3: Work Unit Accountability

Teams are another stage on the route to organizational accountability. At this stage, the success of the team is more important than any particular individual's success. People on the team assist each other in being successful. Competition among team members is lower, but territorialism between teams is still high.

Coordination is high within the team and ineffective between functional areas, resulting in wasted human and technical resources. Teams address individual poor performance and behaviors that keep the team

---

1. Judith M. Bardwick presents a thought-provoking analysis of the dangers of entitlement in her book, *Danger in the Comfort Zone*, American Management Association, 1991.

---

from being successful. Decisions are made without considering the impact on the rest of the organization outside the team and its members.

Level 4: Cross-Functional Accountability

At this level of accountability, business outcomes determine the makeup of the team to get the job done regardless of function. Decisions are made to include as many functions or departments as are affected. Achieving defined outcomes is more important than the success of any one team or individual.

Coordination among teams and individuals is high. Territorialism doesn't exist and individual competition is minimal. Human and technical resources are shared effectively across functional areas, reducing duplication and costs as well as increasing operational effectiveness.

Level 5: Organizational Accountability

This level is similar to Level 4 but represents a further refinement. Business outcomes still drive performance and decision making, but they now include cross-divisional decisions, knowledge sharing, and sharing of resources. All levels of the organization are accountable to each other, creating a "fluid" organization. Any person can act as the leader to any other person, regardless of position, when it is necessary for accomplishing business outcomes.

Clearly, *organizational* accountability cannot possibly be achieved by merely increasing *personal* accountability. Focusing individual commitments and individual actions will not address many of the critical issues, preventing effective performance execution that is critical for optimizing accountability and results.

Figure 1-3 can help you identify the accountability level at which your organization is currently operating. Compare your personal level of accountability to the rest of your organization. If you notice a significant gap, you may be interested in conducting a more in-depth assessment of accountability for yourself or your organization. You can take the Situational Action Inventory, developed by John Jones and Mark Samuel to assess individual accountability according to the Accountability Continuum. (For more information on personal or organizational assessments, contact us at info@impaqcorp.com.)

Figure 1-3: Levels of Accountability

LEVEL 1: ENTITLEMENT

Cultural Characteristics
- Chaotic
- Low morale
- Low trust
- Low support
- Apathetic/No involvement
- Minimal communication
- High resistance to change
- Conflicts are personality oriented
- Little direction from leadership
- No recognition for results

Performance Characteristics
- No operational standards
- Policies aren't defined or maintained
- Poor performance is accepted
- Coordination is poor
- Wasted human/technical resources
- Decisions aren't made
- Projects are over-budget and over-time

LEVEL 2: INDIVIDUAL ACCOUNTABILITY

Cultural Characteristics
- Low support
- High resistance to change
- Highly competitive between team members
- High territorialism
- Conflicts driven by competition
- Power driven
- Communication is fragmented
- Fear of reprimands
- Low involvement
- Individuals are recognized for effort and results

Performance Characteristics
- Policies are maintained
- Operational procedures are defined, with consequences
- Poor performance is addressed
- Coordination is poor
- Duplication of human and technical resources
- Decisions are political and position-driven
- Projects are over-budget and over-time
- Breakdowns between functional areas and line and between management and employees
- Individual performance undermines organizational results

Figure 1-3: Levels of Accountability

LEVEL 3: WORK UNIT ACCOUNTABILITY

Cultural Characteristics

- Support is high within the team
- Medium level of trust
- Highly competitive between functional teams and departments
- Cross-functional territorialism
- Departmental conflicts
- Communication fragmented
- We/they attitude
- Medium involvement
- Individuals and teams are recognized for results

Performance Characteristics

- Policies are maintained
- Operational procedures defined with consequences
- Poor performance is addressed by team and leader
- Resources aren't shared, causing duplication
- Coordination between functional areas break down
- Decisions don't include affected parties and need to be remade or fail
- Global projects are over-budget and overtime
- Team performance undermines organizational results

LEVEL 4: CROSS-FUNCTIONAL ACCOUNTABILITY

Cultural Characteristics

- Confusion about direction based on misinformation
- Conflicts between levels within organization
- Communication blocked
- High involvement of middle management and nonmanagement
- High support between functions and within teams
- Medium to high morale
- Individuals and teams are recognized for results

Performance Characteristics

- Policies are maintained
- Operational procedures are defined with consequences
- Poor performance handled by team and leader—except at upper management level where nonperformance is tolerated
- Resources are shared
- Coordination between functional areas is high and seamless
- Decisions include affected cross-functional parties, but may break down between levels
- Projects are held up by lack of decisions from management
- Organizational performance is undermined by friction between levels in the organization

Figure 1-3: Levels of Accountability

LEVEL 5: ORGANIZATIONAL ACCOUNTABILITY

Cultural Characteristics

- Clear leadership direction
- High communication and information flow
- Decisions are made at all levels and include all functions
- Direction is clear and updated regularly
- Conflicts resolved quickly
- High involvement of execs, middle managers, and nonmanagement in moving the organization forward to achieve business outcomes
- High support between levels and functions and within teams
- Medium to high morale
- Individuals and teams are recognized for results

Performance Characteristics

- Policies are maintained
- Operational procedures are defined, with consequences
- Poor performance is addressed
- Resources are shared
- Coordination is high and seamless
- Decisions include affected cross-functional parties and appropriate levels of the organization
- Projects are effectively monitored and decisions made at the appropriate levels to assure continuous progress
- Organizational performance is assured by the "fluid" involvement of the appropriate levels of the organization

Principles for Increasing Organizational Accountability

1. Accountability increases one level at a time.

Back in 1994, at the height of "teams" as a popular change effort, I worked with an organization that decided moving to a team-based culture would increase performance in the organization. The problem was that, up until that point, there had been no consequences for *individual* nonperformance.

For a while, the energy in the organization improved in response to the promise of working together in teamwork. However, after a few months, the nonperformers still didn't perform, and now they blamed the team for the lack of results. Without the organization's strength to foster individual accountability, it was hard to maintain team-based accountability.

We have found that it takes six months to a year to solidify each new level. However, in times of crisis, the organization's culture has an opportunity to skip a level of accountability. Unfortunately, this

---

opportunity is rarely seized because people are more inclined to revert to a lower level of accountability during a crisis, in the same way that people will often withdraw when they are in a state of fear. Once people determine that they are not at risk, they may then skip a level, exhibiting an unusual degree of accountability. We often see this within communities when an earthquake or some other natural disaster has occurred.

Apart from the unusual circumstances brought on by a crisis, skipping a level of accountability is rarely successful or lasting. One reason many improvement programs fail to stick is that they ignore the evolution of accountability. That's why people who meet to solve problems as a cross-functional team often resume territorial behavior when they return to their work units.

2. As levels of accountability increase, performance and behavioral expectations increase.

When I was twelve years old, I played on a little league team that was expected to win the championship. We had the best individual ball players of any team. Unfortunately, every team member wanted to be the "star" of the team. So batters would swing for home runs, infielders would run into each other trying to get to the ball first, and outfielders would overthrow the ball trying to throw runners out. Frustrated and probably embarrassed by the losses we experienced, the coach decided to practice us harder and concentrate on our catching, batting, and throwing skills. Despite this effort, we still lost games because our attitude and behavior of trying to be the "stars" never changed.

We not only needed to be accountable for performing our skills at the highest level, we also had to be accountable for *performance execution*. Performance execution includes the actions, interactions, behaviors, and communication necessary to achieve business outcomes. It implies linkage between people to achieve desired outcomes. In the case of our team, it included *communicating, coordinating,* and *cooperating* with one another at the highest levels if we were going to win games. By the time the coach figured out that our "star" attitude was the problem, the season was over. We ran out of time and ended the year with a losing record.

As levels of accountability increase, it becomes less acceptable to accomplish individual performance goals without considering the effect on other people in the organization who need to accomplish their goals. When there is cross-functional accountability, each person must communicate, coordinate, and make decisions with people in other functions in order to accomplish the organization's goals.

3. The further removed an individual is from the organization's current level of accountability, the greater the pressure will be for that person to leave the organization.

This is true whether an individual's level of accountability is higher than or lower than that of the organization.

For example, a division of a large manufacturing organization suffered from low performance and low morale. The employee population was comprised of people who had been on the job for fifteen years and had an "entitlement" attitude about their job. Coming to work, putting in time, and doing the least possible to get the job done was the name of the game. Management, in an attempt to improve performance and morale, hired new people who were committed to teamwork, continuous improvement, and maintaining a positive attitude toward the company.

After six months, most of these new employees quit the job saying, "I can't be successful in an environment that is so negative and counterproductive." The organization wasn't at a high enough level of accountability for the employees to stay. Organizations with a low level of accountability not only suffer from low performance and morale, but they can end up losing their top performers who become frustrated and leave.

The next year, the organization embarked on a process to increase accountability in the organization. Team standards were created, continuous improvement processes were established, and agreements were created to improve the relationship between management and employees. Although most of the employees welcomed this change, there were a few longstanding employees who resisted the change. Within a year, many of those people left the company (mostly voluntarily), finding themselves struggling to keep up and not having the power to negate the increase in accountability.

Not everyone fits in with their organization. When people are accountable, they won't fit into an organization of *entitlement* (Level 1). Likewise, people with an attitude of *individual accountability* (Level 2) won't fit into an organization that has a high level of cross-functional accountability.

Conclusion: What You Can Do Now

What is the current level of accountability in your organization? Your team? What attitudes and behaviors need to change for your organization to increase its level of accountability and performance? What do you need to do differently to increase your own personal level of accountability? What would be the advantages of making these changes?

CHAPTER 2

CREATE AN ACCOUNTABLE CULTURE: STOP AVOIDING THE REAL ISSUES!

MYTH: Culture affects people issues more than it affects business outcomes.

TRUTH: The achievement of business outcomes depends on the culture in which people work together to produce results.

YOU NEED ONLY LOOK AT ORGANIZATIONAL BREAKDOWNS AND FAILURES to see that *culture* is anything but a "soft" issue. For example, when one organization lost its competitive edge because it didn't release its new product in time to head off the competition, the issue was cultural, not technical. The organization had a culture of independence where people didn't show up to meetings on time, people constantly checked their e-mails using Blackberries, and some would leave the meetings before they were concluded, resulting in a lack of decision making and taking action necessary to complete the new product line.

A conflict averse organization lost tremendous market share when it didn't deal with the conflicts between the sales department and manufacturing, resulting in huge backlogs, inaccurate order completion, and dissatisfied customers.

Here's a third example: a healthcare organization went out of business due to reductions in revenue and increased costs, when its clinical practitioners spent more time blaming each other's departments for patient care issues rather than improving productivity and patient satisfaction.

Although it is thought that culture represents the "soft" issues of an organization, there is nothing soft about culture when it keeps you from achieving your business outcomes. However, addressing the "soft" issues in a way that makes a meaningful difference cannot always be achieved in the classroom by learning more skills. We need to learn from the performing arts—e.g., dance companies, theatrical groups, and athletic teams. They depend on the "soft" issues of cooperation, communication, and teamwork to ensure a flawless performance.

What is the correlation between culture and business results when you think of organizations such as General Motors, Toyota, Apple Computer, Hewlett-Packard, Nordstroms, and Sears? In what ways does your organization's culture impact your business results?

Culture: The Backbone of an Organization

Organizational culture is simply the way people function together in order to achieve their desired business outcomes.

Although organizational culture is treated as a soft issue, it may be the single most important factor in an organization's ability to achieve its desired business outcomes. In the frustration of doing everything "right" and not achieving desired results, we tend to initiate a frenzy of change efforts. We change our structure, reengineer our systems, provide more training, and do more planning—and still we fail to achieve the results we're after.

The culture of an organization involves more than the style, attitude, communication, and skill of its managers and employees. The reason it has been treated as a soft issue is that it seems to affect people and morale more than it affects business results. Consequently, we debate which culture is best—team-based, self-directed, empowered, diverse, or something else—without reflecting on the primary purpose of any culture, which is to achieve the business outcomes.

The problem is that we develop isolated programs to change the organizational culture in order to satisfy the "human element," while demanding harsh changes in the workplace, such as downsizing and cost cutting, in order to achieve our business results. The reality is that culture directly affects the organization's profitability and competitive edge in the marketplace to a degree that most people have failed to appreciate.

Unfortunately, the cultures of most organizations today are based on a victim orientation of ignoring problems, blaming others for mistakes, rationalizing inflexibility, resisting the need to change and/or improve, and hiding from those who are going to hold them accountable.

> The culture represents the fabric of the organization. You can't create a functional raincoat out of an evening gown without changing the fabric. It may look like a raincoat and it may be worn like a raincoat, but we have only to wear it out in the rain to know that it won't function as a raincoat. The same holds true for organizations.

Michael Hammer describes this well in his book *Beyond Reengineering*: "Despite their many differences, there are great similarities across most contemporary corporate cultures. Certain themes resonate almost everywhere: avoiding blame and responsibility, treating co-workers as competitors, feeling entitled, and not feeling intense and committed."[1]

The culture represents the fabric of the organization. You can't create a functional raincoat out of an evening gown without changing the fabric. It may look like a raincoat and it may be worn like a raincoat, but we have only to wear it out in the rain to know that it won't function as a raincoat. The same holds true for organizations. You can restructure your organization into teams, provide people with team awareness and skills through team training, and even change your compensation to a team-based structure, and still not have people function as a team that achieves the results you want.

It involves more than the attitudes, skills, and styles of people as

1. Michael Hammer, *Beyond Reengineering: How the Process-Center Is Changing Our Work and Our Lives*, Harper & Row, 1996.

individuals: it involves a *collective mind-set* and the linkage between people in the form of *behavior patterns* that support that collective mind-set. These behavior patterns between people represent "habits of performance execution" that result in business outcomes. Performance execution is comprised of *habits* that represent the automatic behavior demonstrated on a consistent basis in the organization. Some common habits of performance execution include:

- How managers typically deal with nonperformance
- How effectively information is shared between departments
- How decisions are made that include the impacted departments and people

Just as it is critical for a football team to determine the kind of performance execution—to be a passing team or a running team—necessary to win ball games, organizations need to determine the ideal habits of performance execution to achieve optimal business results. These habits form the "hows" of the culture, as represented by some of the following processes:

- How information is shared between levels and departments to ensure effective operations
- How coordination of activities is handled between departments
- How conflict is treated and addressed
- How decisions are made that impact various individuals and departments
- How nonperformance is handled within a team and by management
- How people are developed according to the intention and future needs of the organization
- How people are recognized on a daily basis as opposed to "awards of the month"
- How problems are surfaced and quickly resolved
- How resources are shared between projects

Effective habits of performance execution help an organization: meet customer needs, keep costs low, support high productivity, and change to achieve business outcomes. Examples of positive habits of performance execution are:

- Include the right people when making a decision to prevent a breakdown or duplication of effort

- Coach nonperformers immediately, with clear consequences to reduce the time spent in ineffective performance

- Communicate direction and change effectively to ensure swift action and involvement by those doing the implementing

Just as *effective* habits of performance execution support the organization's success, *dysfunctional* habits of performance execution undermine the organization's effectiveness and result in wasted resources, poor customer service, higher costs, lower productivity, and inconsistent quality. Some of these dysfunctional habits of performance execution include:

- Not surfacing project breakdowns when milestones aren't being met

- Avoiding conflict and hoping the problem will go away

- Not communicating expectations clearly, causing rework, wasted effort, and a lack of responsiveness to customers

- Meetings where information is shared, but where decisions aren't made and actions aren't taken to make progress on priorities

These habits of performance execution are generally automatic responses that people demonstrate in an organization, regardless of their positions or functions. As a result, they can be considered the "habits" of an organization. The organization's culture is the sum total of its habits, effective and ineffective.

Dysfunctional habits represent the internal, almost invisible barriers of an organization. Most dysfunctional habits of an organization are based on fear and the absence of trust. Kathleen Ryan and Daniel Oestreich discuss the impact of fear in their book *Driving Fear Out of the Workplace*, claiming, "We see fear as an increasingly visible background phenomenon that undermines the commitment, motivation, and confidence of people at work."[2]

Fear undermines performance in a way that prevents organizations from achieving high performance and breakthrough results. It is the fear of making mistakes, of speaking out and being reprimanded for it, and of making others feel uncomfortable that causes breakdowns in coordinating projects, making critical decisions, and taking initiative to solve problems that have surfaced. Developing an accountable organization means that we are constantly surfacing the dysfunctional "habits" of performance and communication, identifying the fear associated with those habits, and developing new "habits" that promote greater levels of trust and high performance.

Although these habits of performance execution appear to be the soft issues that affect only the morale, they are critical elements directly impacting the organization's performance, efficiency, reputation with customers, and profitability. Figure 2-1 illustrates the consequences of dysfunctional patterns of behavior, especially with regard to profitability, in several different types of organizations.

Spineless Leadership Breeds Victimization

Just as it takes courage to tell the truth when you have to deliver "bad" news, it takes courage to lead with accountability. It is easy for managers to complain that employees aren't taking initiative, are wasting time on useless activities, and are unwilling to put in the effort to achieve excellence. Here's what happens when leaders fail to be accountable:

- When leadership doesn't have the courage to identify and articulate a clear direction for the future (demonstrated by the focus of a few priorities), employees waste time on meaningless activities and meetings, looking busy but not actually making progress.

- When leaders don't have the courage to make decisions, employees remain paralyzed, either in conflict or awaiting approval.

2. Kathleen D. Ryan and Daniel K. Oestreich, *Driving Fear Out of the Workplace*, Jossey-Bass, 1998.

- When leaders fail to demonstrate the courage to coach and deal with nonperformers, employees quickly learn that hard work and dedication to excellence is neither respected nor recognized.

Figure 2-1: Dysfunctional Patterns of Behavior

Topic: *Coordination in a Biomedical Organization*

Dysfunctional Pattern of Behavior:
Each project manager developed isolated plans for completing his or her part of the project without strategizing or coordinating plans with those involved in other parts of the project.

Result on Business Outcomes:
Fragmented activities caused breakdowns that delayed the completion of the project by over two years. The result was a new product that was late to market and millions of dollars in wasted resources, not to mention opportunity loss.

Note: The project was scrapped and restarted with the same team of project managers. This time a new system of coordination was implemented when the project was initiated. The new product was developed ahead of the scheduled completion date.

Topic: *Dealing with Nonperformers in a Financial Institution*

Dysfunctional Pattern of Behavior:
In support of a polite "culture" emphasizing "fairness" and comfort, there were no consequences for employees or managers who did not perform.

Result on Business Outcomes:
Customer satisfaction dropped as competition increased, resulting in reduced market share. Needing to reduce costs, severance was offered. The organization lost top performers who knew they could get employed elsewhere. The poorly performing employees (concerned about finding new jobs) stayed, costing the organization millions in lost market share, the expense of laying off employees, and the loss of customer confidence and satisfaction.

Note: An electronics firm facing the same dilemma announced that performance/customer satisfaction needed to improve or employees would be cut by 40%. Managers coached people to higher levels of performance and coached nonperformers out of the organization. Result: profits increased and needed cuts amounted to only 8%.

Figure 2-1: Dysfunctional Patterns of Behavior

Topic: *Making Decisions in a Healthcare Organization Managing Multiple Medical Centers*

Dysfunctional Pattern of Behavior:
After empowering a committee to develop a new system for improving performance, no process was in place for making decisions to implement the performance improvement system by top management, middle management, or the individual medical centers.

Result on Business Outcomes:
Five employees spent nine months researching, developing, and testing a new performance improvement system within the organization. While they could demonstrate measurable results from their pilot programs, the executive team wasn't able to make a unified decision to implement the improvement system. The initiative was aborted.

Note: As a result, more than $600,000 was wasted in employee time and in the purchase of the recommended improvement system that was piloted. Some of the wasted money was offset by the success of the pilots, but did not make up for the opportunities lost by the lack of implementation.

Topic: *Dealing with Conflict in a Division of a Petroleum Company*

Dysfunctional Pattern of Behavior:
When people at the same level are in conflict, it is customary for those involved to ignore one another and bring their issues to upper management for resolution. This took too long and fragmented decisions were made that created new conflicts.

Result on Business Outcomes:
Based on unresolved conflicts over operational issues between departments, operational systems broke down and production levels were lower than the other divisions within the company. Morale was also negatively impacted by the unresolved disagreements between managers that affected employees.

Note: After developing the process for resolving conflicts without going to upper management, 55% of all unresolved conflicts were completely resolved within six months. One year later, the same division had the highest levels of production and morale.

- When leaders don't demonstrate the courage to admit making mistakes, then employees also hide their mistakes and their failing projects.

- When leaders avoid addressing concerns, employees refuse to take continuous improvement, performance appraisal, and professional development seriously.

In general, when leadership runs away from taking accountability, employees respond in kind.

Old Habits Die Hard: A Case Study

A division of a major petroleum company in Venezuela needed to cut costs and improve its productivity in order to compete in the new global market. It was clear that to cut costs successfully, the division had to share resources more effectively. The management team decided it was necessary to restructure the organization, from centralized departments to cross-functional business units. This required changing the organization into a team-based culture. The previously autonomous departments were Maintenance, Operations, and Technical Services, which were restructured into five business units. To support the team structure, people received training in the value of teamwork and in the skills required of a team-based culture.

When centralized, the organization had relied on two trucks from the maintenance department to serve all five of its operating plants. With the decentralization, each business unit contained its own maintenance function. But there were still only two trucks. So the business unit managers (all of whom supported and were skilled in the new team structure) met to determine which units would get the trucks and how they could serve the needs of those units who wouldn't get the trucks. They reverted back to their old mindset of "management by control" and their old habit of fighting one another, and resulted in an argumentative stalemate that lasted three weeks. Their final decision was that the only way to solve the problem was to purchase three more trucks so that each business unit could have its own truck. Instead of cutting costs, they *increased* them!

As Stephen Covey pointed out so forcefully in his excellent book, *The Seven Habits of Highly Effective People*, habits can be learned and unlearned, but breaking deeply embedded habits takes a tremendous effort.[3] The business unit managers were still operating from the old culture of *controlling* and

3. Stephen R. Covey, *The Seven Habits of Highly Effective People*, Simon & Schuster, 1989.

fighting for resources, even though they were the ones who suggested and supported the new team-based organization. The direction was clear, the organization had been restructured, and the technical processes had been reengineered. But because people continued to operate from their old culture, their sincerest efforts were undermined or sabotaged. Their ultimate "solution" was completely inconsistent with the organization's goal of cutting costs by sharing resources more effectively.

Developing New Habits of Performance Execution

People don't usually change habits by reading a book, taking a class, or gaining new information. If it were that easy, people wouldn't have so much trouble losing weight, quitting smoking, or reducing alcohol consumption. To change a habit, you must replace the old habit with a new one. It isn't enough to teach people new skills about eating; instead, we must provide them with a *system* for eating that is repetitive so that over time their new *habit* of eating takes over automatically.

You may have experienced an organization where the habit for resolving conflict is to talk behind people's backs. When the issue finally reaches the attention of the person targeted, the one who started the rumor denies any involvement. People attend workshops on managing conflict in which they practice new communication skills, body language, and active listening. Also, they may learn people's styles so that they can become more understanding when they are in conflict. While some may apply their new skills, many return to the workplace and resume their old habits of behavior. So when a conflict surfaces, they still don't talk. They just become more effective at blaming each other behind each other's backs. If anything, the workshops have enabled them to blame the other person's style more convincingly, using their new communication skills to do so.

Five Steps to Create Organizational Accountability

Developing a culture that produces breakthrough results involves more than changing behaviors or attitudes, or adding new skills to the workforce. It involves *developing new habits of performance execution*. Although it make take years to change all the bad habits of an organization, with focused attention and deliberate methodology it only requires three to six months to change enough significant habits to achieve measurable impact on an organization's desired business outcomes.

Introduce a New Mind-set

People are familiar with the way things have always been done and will take any change effort and impose past performance, behavioral, and attitudinal norms to the change. This is natural. When we focus our attention on learning the new technology, new structure, or new process, we fail to address the person's old ways of thinking and the habits that go with that mind-set.

For instance, a service-based organization was organized into functional departments. Each functional department had its own priorities and goals. However, based on satisfying customer needs, the different functional departments had to work closely together coordinating their efforts. When they failed to do so, which happened more often than not, delays took place, costs increased, and customers complained. In addition, conflicts grew between the functional departments as they "blamed" each other for the breakdowns.

To resolve this issue, the organization restructured into "process teams" that included team members from each of the functional departments. Each process team had a leader, but the team members still reported to their manager of the functional department from which they came. Do you think that the restructure resolved the issue of coordination breakdowns and unresolved conflicts? No. They went into the "new" organization with the same "mind-set" as before. Their allegiance was still to their functional department.

When any change is implemented in an organization, here's what you need to do:

- You must start by *clarifying the new mind-set* in terms of expanding roles and new responsibilities.

- You must also *identify how the relationships in the organization may be altered* based on the change and desired outcomes being accomplished.

- Finally, you must *clarify any new expectations* for improved performance or productivity as a result of the change you are implementing.

If you don't do these things, people will perform and communicate in their old ways decreasing the impact of the change. (Details about changing mind-set are given in chapter 6.)

Step 2

Identify and Reverse Dysfunctional Habits of Performance Execution

The organization needs to identify the "bad" habits of performance execution that have kept it from achieving its previous desired outcomes. Habits of performance execution refer to the behaviors that link one person or group to another in order to accomplish performance expectations. It also must identify those habits of performance execution that were effective in achieving *previous* desired outcomes, but that probably won't work to achieve the *new desired* outcomes.

Once the dysfunctional habits have been identified, it is necessary to develop descriptions of the desired habits so that people can get a true sense of the new ways of successful functioning in the organization. We refer to these successful ways of functioning as "success factors of performance execution." For example, one leadership team created a success factor stating: "When you are experiencing conflict with another manager, go to him or her directly to create a resolution that best meets the needs of the organization as well as the needs of each department represented in the conflict."

This was a dramatic change from what had been the team members' habitual behavior of going to *upper* management to resolve the conflict.

The new habits of behavior must then be implemented at each level (which will be discussed in chapter 3). This is one of the most important steps in creating a culture of accountability, because *accountability requires linkages among people.* This step details the desired expectations for the kinds of linkage necessary for organizational success. (Developing success factors of performance execution is detailed in chapter 8.)

Measure the Effectiveness of the New Habits of Performance Execution

To successfully change a habit, you must *repeat* the new habit until it becomes *automatic* behavior. Although most organizations use measurement to evaluate results, the first purpose of measurement is *focus*. What you measure, you focus on.

For example, top athletes measure how much water they drink, the quantities and combinations of food they eat, and how much they sleep. This doesn't evaluate their skill or performance as an athlete, but it does keep them *focused* on the aspects of performance execution that lead to top performance.

We need to do the same in organizations. Sometimes performance execution is measured in numbers, but other times it is simply a tracking system or a subjective score. Before recording in a studio, a band needs to be as "tight" as possible. This isn't measured in numbers, but is "measured" subjectively looking for consistency and listening for unison.

The first part of measurement is to determine if people are using the new habits (success factors) of performance execution. The second part is to measure the impact of the success factors of performance execution on desired business outcomes. New behaviors may be successful in terms of implementation, but the results may be counterproductive according to the stated vision and desired business outcomes. If new habits aren't working, the reality may be that people haven't actually tried them. An organization may spend more time and resources developing new ones rather than effectively implementing the existing ones. (Measuring habits of performance execution is discussed in more detail in chapter 8.)

Step 4

Establish Recovery Systems Prior to Implementation

This is the most important step for ensuring sustained results. There are two natural tendencies that cause organizations to fail:

- The tendency to try something new, discover it doesn't work the first time around, and then give up, reverting to the old, comfortable way of doing things.

- The tendency to adopt the new habit of behavior, then be surprised by a crisis situation and revert back to the old habit.

As will be discussed in the chapter 3, it is vital that you don't expect perfection. Instead, you must be prepared with a *recovery strategy* so that you can act when a crisis occurs, when you regress to old habits of behavior, or when you discover that the new behavior isn't working as well as desired. Recovery allows you to continue making progress even when mistakes arise or flaws are discovered.

Step 5

Recognize Results and People

An accountable organization not only recognizes mistakes, but also recognizes success. It's important to take ownership for success, learn from success, and share the learning in order to sustain and expand improvements. Otherwise, whereas recognition often has the effect of making people feel good, it has a greater purpose in creating an accountable organization: it serves to *solidify the new mind-set and behaviors* that are producing results.

This opportunity is missed when organizations fail to provide people with sufficient feedback or recognition regarding actual results before moving on to a new goal. Inadequate feedback sends a message to employees that the results achieved weren't important. Why, then, would they want to invest their energy in the next project to improve the organization?

You miss another opportunity when you give recognition to people's efforts without linking their efforts to the results of the change. When you do that, they experience recognition as empty and meaningless.

Successful recognition involves two steps:

1. *Recognize the impact that eliminating dysfunctional habits had on the organization's business outcomes.* For instance, a team feels more valued for its contribution knowing that by resolving conflicts it eliminated five inefficient processes that saved the organization fifty hours of employee time and $20,000 per week in misuse of equipment.

2. *Recognize people's efforts when appropriate, and link them to the actual improvements and progress made by the organization.* For instance, one organization created a celebration lunch each month to recognize teams that achieved breakthrough results. At the celebration, teams would acknowledge the people (inside and outside of the team) that contributed to achieving the stellar results.

Effective recognition reinforces that the elimination of dysfunctional habits and the development of new ones were meaningful.

THREE TRAPS OF INEFFECTIVE LEADERSHIP

> **MYTH:** Task-oriented leaders who are constantly busy produce successful results.
>
> **TRUTH:** Leaders who focus more on meaningful priorities and less on activity produce successful results.

A S THE BRITISH WRITER SAMUEL JOHNSON NOTED so astutely in the 18th century, "Nothing will ever be attempted if all possible objections must be first overcome." The reason so many projects fail is because management tries to *perfect* the plan prior to implementation. Often, managers rationalize their drive for perfection by insisting that they need to ensure buy-in, and they argue that people won't buy-in until the plan is perfect.

Then, when the organization can't afford to spend more time on the plan, management goes ahead and communicates the implementation strategy, only to run up against resistance and negativity. In an effort to make people comfortable, management decides to *study* the problem and *plan further* in order to get less resistance, and the implementation is delayed until the plan is finally deemed "perfect." But there will always be resistance.

Then, when implementation fails, people who are involved with the implementation (not the planning) are blamed for not achieving the desired results. Management moves to the next goal or project, while employees are still reeling from the current effort. Their resistance to future change strategies and goals is now that much stronger. You rarely achieve your desired outcomes when the outcomes become a slave to the process.

The brutality of autocratic and dictatorial leadership that marked much of the first half of the last century provoked the development of a series of bad leadership habits that continue to plague organizations and employees to this day. The changes that are required may seem at first glance to herald a return to antiquated, autocratic leadership. But on closer inspection, it will be obvious that accountability-based leadership not only increases the achievement of *business outcomes* but also *improves employee morale and job satisfaction*. To develop accountable and effective organizations, you must follow three guidelines:

1. Focus on the desired outcome rather than on the process.

2. Create safety, not comfort.

3. Focus on recovery, not on perfection.

Each of these guidelines is discussed in detail in the rest of this chapter.

Guideline #1:
Focus on the Desired Outcome Rather Than on the Process

Dilbert's Wally takes process to new heights of absurdity with something he calls "Process Pride": "It all started when I realized I have no impact on earnings. Obviously, I can't take pride in the results of my work. But I need pride. Otherwise, how could I maintain my high level of morale? So I learned to take pride in my processes instead of in my results. Everything I do is still pointless, but I'm very proud of the way I do it."

There was a time when it was necessary to be process-oriented. Prior to the Quality Movement, decisions were made autocratically by management without including input from affected employees. This caused frustration and resistance among employees and resulted in inefficient operational systems.

The Quality Movement recognized the need for employees to become directly involved in changing the operational systems for which they were responsible. Unfortunately, employees didn't have the problem-solving and decision-making skills required to improve operational systems. Additionally, management had difficulty relinquishing control, which resulted in continued micromanagement of employees.

To remedy both of these problems, the Quality Movement emphasized specific processes aimed at keeping management from micromanaging and guiding the employees in effective problem solving and decision making. By necessity, everyone became process-oriented. This was the most effective way to break the old patterns of autocratic management and dependent employees.

Some organizations have become so process-oriented that they fail to achieve business results. An executive from a healthcare organization described it this way, "In our organization, we can't seem to make a decision because we are so process-oriented and inclusive. Trying to satisfy everyone's internal needs causes us to settle for mediocre solutions that aren't responsive to the needs of our customers. The process itself has become more important than serving our customer."

Beware the Three Traps of Ineffective Leadership

Trap #1: Seek the perfect process and get stuck in analysis paralysis.

How often have you seen task forces or committees bogged down for months trying in vain to reach consensus? Maybe you've witnessed a group arguing ad nauseam over a process issue like: "Do you collect information by doing a survey or by doing interviews?" The truth is, there is no single perfect process; rather, there are many possible routes to the same end. Unless you choose one and start moving toward the goal, you will never arrive. The only way to fail is to fail to move.

> The only way to fail is to fail to move.

For example, a management team from a pharmaceutical company was meeting to make a decision about moving forward on a project. The team was missing one person, but it was efficient in making its decision to move forward. After a break in the meeting, the missing person showed up. He was appalled that the team made the decision without his input. He challenged the decision and asked to discuss it more.

Did he have new information that would change the decision? No. Did he have a new idea that would change the decision? No. Did he agree with the decision made? Yes. So, why did he want to discuss the decision? Because he wasn't part of the original discussion.

When I asked the team if it had a pattern of rehashing decisions in order to maintain a process where everyone had to have their say, the team responded, "Yes, all the time."

Of course, trust can break down fast when the process of making decisions excludes people's input. However, trust can also break down when a team can't make decisions in a responsive way to get results, because team members take it personally if a decision is made without them.

Trap #2: The desired progress to achieve results comes to a halt because of disagreements regarding the purpose or direction of the goal or project.

A work unit can easily become polarized or a project team can get stuck due to confusion or disagreement about its purpose or goal. As soon as we stop moving toward our outcome, the entire project is at risk.

For example, I was once called on to work with a dysfunctional work unit that had been given the charter to improve quality while reducing costs. One part of the unit determined that replacing old, damaged equipment with new equipment would result in greater efficiency and higher customer satisfaction. Another part resisted this solution because it would involve spending money. As a result, no suggestions for improvement came from this work unit for three years. That is when I was called in!

Trap #3: We fail to hold people accountable when they are not achieving the outcome.

Almost everyone knows of chronic nonperformers who escape corrective action by blaming the imperfect processes used by the organization. Managers, in turn, think that they need to perfect the processes before they can deal with the nonperformer. Figure 3-1 illustrates how focus on processes decreases as an organization becomes more accountable, so that it can focus more on the desired outcome.

As organizations move from entitlement toward accountability, they focus more on the outcome than on the process.

For example, think back to when you first learned how to drive a car.

Figure 3-1:
The Process/Outcome Continuum

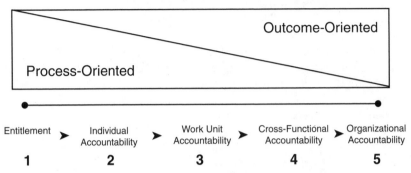

Entitlement	Individual Accountability	Work Unit Accountability	Cross-Functional Accountability	Organizational Accountability
1	2	3	4	5

Do you remember where your focus was? If you're like most people, your eyes focused on the road immediately in front of the car, while your mind focused on the foot action; on how much pressure was needed on the gas pedal, the clutch, and the brake pedal; and on the activities of your hands on the steering wheel. You were much more alert about the process of driving than you've ever been since. You thought little about your destination. In fact, your field of vision was limited to perhaps the end of the block.

An important part of driver education is to train the driver to focus on the *big picture*—where you are going—while remaining aware of the process of driving. If you focus exclusively on the *process*, you are in danger of having an accident. With practice, of course, the process of driving becomes automatic. It is no longer "front of mind."

Similarly, shifting focus back and forth from the current operational environment to the future desired outcome is ideal for leading organizations. If we're driving across the country, we keep checking the map to make sure we're proceeding toward our ultimate destination. If we're behind schedule, we adjust our process by not stopping as often, changing to a less scenic route, or speeding up. When we're not progressing according to plan, we need to examine the process, not for the purpose of perfecting it, but to modify it in order to achieve the desired outcome.

We tend to lose sight of our destination and get stuck analyzing the process. We can argue endlessly about which fast food restaurant to stop at on the highway, and lose sight of the fact that we are going to miss our appointment.

For a cable company, survival meant increasing market share. Each department, regardless of function, was given shared responsibility to increase market share. It was determined that costs had to be cut so prices could be more competitive. Also, quality service and responsiveness had to improve in order to increase customer satisfaction. Finally, sales efforts had to increase in order to turn nonusers into customers. Each department had different and seemingly unrelated functions. Consequently, an analysis was conducted to determine how the specific functions of each department related to market share.

Based on this analysis, each department developed improvement goals designed to increase market share. If a department worked only on meeting its own self-serving goals, it was held accountable by the management team and redirected to the outcome of increasing market share. Measurements were put into place and tracked weekly to determine the progress made by each department and to uncover obstacles that needed to be removed.

Within six months, all of the departments were ahead of schedule on their improvement efforts, and market share and revenue exceeded their annual target outcome.

Guideline #2: Create Safety, Not Comfort

The words *safety* and *comfort* are often used synonymously. But they are different words with different meanings. In an accountable organization, we strive to create a safe environment, *not* a comfortable one.

Think of the last time that you made a significant paradigm shift in your thinking, attitude, or behavior. Did you make this shift when you were *comfortable* and everything was going smoothly in your life, or when you were *challenged* and wondering how (or if) you would get through it? You experience comfort when you are satisfied with your life. When you love your job, your boss, your relationship at home, and the money you are earning, do you really want to make a change? Why rock the boat? You are generally making changes when a part of your life *isn't working* and you want to make it better.

Sometimes, however, although you aren't satisfied with the way things are, you resist new ways of thinking or new behaviors because you are afraid of the consequences. If the change you are thinking of making would result in the loss of a relationship, the loss of your job, or ridicule, you might think twice before making that change. We might call this kind of change "punishing."

Although you don't choose to modify your behavior when you are comfortable with the way things are, you also don't choose to modify your behavior when you sense that you will be *punished* for doing so. To develop new, effective behaviors, you must feel a sense of "safety" for taking the risks associated with those behaviors. There may be discomfort or even pain involved. But the pain associated with making changes when you feel safe has none of the sense of punishment that is associated with making changes when you do not feel safe.

> In an accountable organization, we strive to create a safe environment, *not* a comfortable one.

The greater your level of safety, the easier it is for you to change old habits. Generally, your level of safety increases with experience. The more often you have modified old habits, successfully moving through your discomfort in the process, the safer you will feel about making subsequent modifications to your behavior.

We've identified three zones of personal transformation:

1. The Punishment Zone

2. The Safety Zone

3. The Comfort Zone

For example, a workshop participant illustrated these three zones of personal transformation when she described her process for learning how to ski. Already a beginning skier, she was quite content to remain at that level. She was *comfortable*. However, her friends, all more advanced skiers, wanted her to ski with them. Nervously, she agreed to try an intermediate slope. Although frightened, she decided she could go down the hill as long as she allowed herself to fall (allowing herself to fall was giving her *safety* to make mistakes and to take the risks associated with the challenge of an intermediate slope). Twelve falls later, she was down the hill in one piece and decided to try it again. This time she made it down with only five falls.

Her comfort zone was increasing as her safety zone increased. If she had stayed comfortable, she would still have been stuck on the "bunny

---

Figure 3-2:
How Safety Affects Behavior

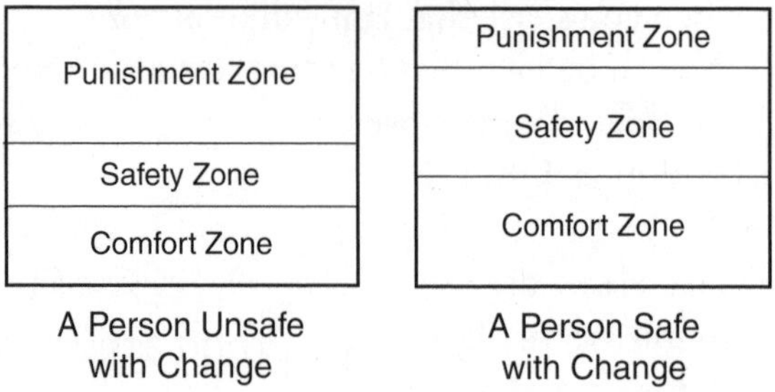

Punishment Zone	Punishment Zone
	Safety Zone
Safety Zone	Comfort Zone
Comfort Zone	
A Person Unsafe with Change	A Person Safe with Change

slopes" and would have felt unsafe as an intermediate skier. If her friends had taken her to one of the advanced slopes, she could have been seriously hurt. Her level of fear in that case would have felt *punishing*. As it was, she worked through the discomfort she felt, took the risk, and increased her safety in skiing. Figure 3-2 illustrates this continuum. When people tend to resist change, they have a small *safety zone* and a large *punishment zone.* This means that any amount of change causes them to feel punished. In contrast, when people are flexible to adapt to change with little resistance, they have a large safety zone, where they are safe to take the risks of change, and a relatively small punishment zone. They don't experience change as punishing, but more as an opportunity for growth.

> When people tend to resist change, they have a small *safety zone* and a large *punishment zone.* This means that any amount of change causes them to feel punished.

Some people have been in the same job for thirty years, had the same co-workers for twenty years and the same supervisor for fifteen years. Their comfort has been firmly established by the stability of the environment. When a restructuring is announced, they automatically feel punished by the prospect of change. They are not accustomed to changes in their working environments. Figure 3-3 illustrates how comfort and safety change as an organization becomes increasingly accountable.

The Demise of the Comfortable Organization

Management generally wants to create a safe environment for employees. This, of course, is appropriate when it relates to the physical environment. And, although it is also appropriate for the cultural environment, the mistake most managers make is to equate "safety" with "comfort." Instead of creating an environment in which it is *safe to take risks*, managers create an environment where *being comfortable is the goal*. However, "real" safety occurs when employees can take real chances and know they will be supported.

> Managers create an environment where *being comfortable is the goal*. However, "real" safety occurs when employees can take real chances and know they will be supported.

Organizations with high levels of comfort rather than safety are generally polite organizations where people don't challenge one another and where conflict is avoided. Decisions are put on hold until it is too late to make a good decision or until crisis takes over. Planning is preferred to taking action, because more risk is involved in taking action. Projects are delayed over and over again, because no one is willing to admit stumbling blocks or obstacles. Moreover, organizations that emphasize comfort also tend to be the most political, making decisions and creating policies based on influence rather than on the need to achieve specific outcomes.

Figure 3-3:
The Comfort/Safety Continuum

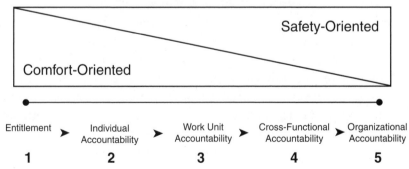

The "comfortable" environment promoted by management is ideally suited for the nonperformers who are never coached and who are transferred to other managers as a "sweeping under the carpet" solution. You know the environment is comfortable when new solutions, projects, or change efforts are put on hold because people are resistant even though the organization's survival is at risk.

Emphasizing comfort can be costly to the organization and result in even greater pain and punishment to the employees. For example, almost thirty years ago in a major California University, a team of typists was directed by management to take computer classes and classes in word processing. The typists resisted the transition to new technology, explaining that they had always used typewriters and that typewriters worked just fine. Management wanted to make them comfortable on the job, so they reversed their decision to require the training. Within five years, the entire department was let go because the people lacked the skills to perform the clerical jobs now demanded by their customers. This was a heavy price to pay for being comfortable. Learning, changing, and growing all require that we experience the discomfort associated with taking the risks to move into uncharted waters.

You can't allow people's natural resistance to change to prevent the process of transformation. Nor is this the time to "empower" others to confront their bad habits or antiquated methods by themselves; doing so will only make them feel alone and abandoned. You must provide *guidance* and *encouragement* to move people through their discomfort, whether expressed as resistance, apathy, hurt, or rebellion.

Guideline #3: Focus on Recovery, Not on Perfection

Focusing on perfection is one of the great diseases of modern organizations. We plan until the plan is perfect. We don't make decisions until we are sure that the decision is the "right" one to make. Ultimately, we end up in analysis paralysis, unable to create the perfect solution. We talk about creating a learning environment, or an environment of continuous improvement, yet in our demand for perfection, we eliminate the safety to make mistakes, to take risks, and to break away from the status quo. We operate with the illusion that once a plan is in place, a decision is made, or a solution is implemented, it can't be adjusted. And we worry that we'll be blamed when it is discovered that our plan, decision, or solution isn't perfect.

Although there are some aspects of planning and decision making that can't be adjusted (such as purchasing of major equipment or building of a new office structure), most plans and decisions must be modified upon implementation. Diane Dreher discusses this in her book, *The Tao of Personal Leadership*, where she notes, "Tao leaders have the strength of bamboo, able to bend, blend with circumstances, adjust to change, and overcome adversity. They can meet any challenge with courage and compassion."[1]

The problem is that when we *expect* perfection, we don't *plan for* imperfection. We are then unprepared when the unexpected takes place. This results in the sort of crisis that causes breakdown.

Some managers fear that creating recovery systems up-front offers an excuse for not performing. However, for most top-performing groups outside the business environment, recovery systems are a way of life. Indeed, they are a direct means for achieving high performance.

For example, consider an NBA championship basketball team, a nationally known theater company, or a military operation. Each one desires perfect performance, but their route to perfection is not only through practicing for perfection, but also through the development of "recovery" systems in case of human error or unexpected incidents. Baseball teams practice their recovery plan when someone drops the ball. Theater companies practice their recovery system when someone forgets his or her lines or when a part of the set malfunctions. Military units develop contingency plans.

In organizations, however, you expect perfection and then blame either the person or the process when breakdown occurs. While everyone is busy blaming each other, the desired business outcome is missed, resulting in yet another failure. Worst of all, you tend to give up, feeling that no amount of time or effort will ever be sufficient to allow for a successful implementation of change.

1. Diane Dreher, *The Tao of Personal Leadership*, Harper & Row, 1996.

Benefits of Creating a Recovery System

Creating a recovery system is a way to stay in the game rather than forfeiting the game altogether. Mistakes will occur and unexpected events will take place, but for the organization that has a recovery system in place, adjustments can be made swiftly and effectively to achieve the desired outcomes. There are three different situations in which recovery systems can be applied:

1. *Recovery is critical for strategic planning efforts.* Many organizations recognize the need for scenario planning or contingency planning in today's changing environment. They create different scenarios based on the variables of external drivers and performance results that could take place.

2. *Recovery is essential for project planning.* As a result of unforeseen circumstances or unresolved problems, projects can be seriously delayed. Usually, project mangers feel a sense of ownership for the project. They don't want to feel a sense of failure.

Consequently, neither the mechanism nor the *safety* exists to surface serious problems that arise. Nor do opportunities exist for others to help create alternative solutions. Decisions can't be made to modify or even to abort the project.

For example, such a situation occurred at one of the largest financial institutions in Canada, where the improvement of computer technology used throughout the organization was a major priority. Millions of dollars were spent on a project to

> Creating a recovery system is a way to stay in the game rather than forfeiting the game altogether.

develop new software and hardware systems. The project was delayed for months, but the delays were not brought to the attention of upper management until it was too late: the delays had reached crisis proportions. After several months and millions of dollars of investment, the project had to be completely aborted.

Even though team members had been concerned about the delays, there were no safety or recovery systems in place to raise the possibility of project failure until millions of dollars had already been spent. A recovery system would have provided the safety and the mechanisms to surface and address serious problems as they arose.

Figure 3-4:
The Perfection/Recovery Continuum

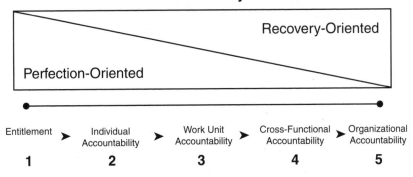

3. *Recovery systems are essential for the improvement of relationships in the workplace.* As organizations become more accountable, they tend to develop agreements among departments, functions, levels, and team members. It is critical that recovery systems are in place so that if agreements are broken, the people involved have a mechanism for discussing and amending them. Otherwise, their anger about the broken agreement may cause them to abandon the agreements completely.

Recovery systems are the key to creating an environment of safety that leads to greater accountability, as shown in figure 3-4. We can solve only those problems that we know about. Without an effective recovery system, problems remain hidden, conflicts remain unresolved, and the resulting culture of nonperformance continues as the norm within the organization.

There is no excuse for failing to improve current processes and functioning when a recovery system is in place. Problems surface before they become a major crisis, and everyone enjoys a sense of satisfaction in overcoming the natural challenges that show up in the work. You will learn more about developing recovery plans in chapter 9.

CHAPTER 4

THE FORMULA TO ACHIEVE BREAKTHROUGHS

MYTH: Empowering people helps them overcome their fear of change.

TRUTH: Guiding people to action helps them *move through* their fear of change.

B EFORE PEOPLE CAN BE MORE ACCOUNTABLE and take action to pursue a new direction, they must have a sense that, like the beginning skier, they are safe enough to risk action that catapults them out of their comfort zone. Otherwise, taking action in a new direction will feel punishing. Paradoxically, the only way for them to increase their level of safety is for them to be accountable and to take action. As our safety increases through taking action, so does our comfort. In the previous chapter, we saw that the skier's comfort and safety increased when she became an intermediate-level skier.

My daughter went through a similar process at the age of eight when she asked me to teach her how to dive at our local pool. We stood at the side of the pool, and I showed her the position for going into the water head-first. She moved into position, stood there for a few moments, then straightened up again.

"Dad," she said, "you dive first to show me what it looks like."

I gladly performed a dive for her. Climbing out of the pool, I said, "Now it's your turn."

She got into position, then quickly straightened up again. "I'm confused," she said. "Please show me again."

I realized she was up against her fear. At this point, I could continue diving and trying to make my daughter feel more comfortable, but I knew that the only way for her to feel safe diving was for her to take the action herself. I urged her to get back into position and just give it a try. I reassured her that I would stand nearby to make sure she was okay.

She gathered up her courage and dove, landing with a splat as she performed her first belly flop. She knew it wasn't the perfect dive, but now she had created the safety to try it again until she could improve her dive to her satisfaction. Safety

> Safety to take risks leads to taking action and being accountable.

to take risks leads to taking action and being accountable. By taking action, we create a new level of safety for ourselves that leads to bigger challenges and changes, as illustrated in figures 4-1 and 4-2.

Being safe to take risks does not mean that you feel no pain or discomfort. On the contrary, the safety zone always involves a degree of discomfort. But instead of fleeing from that discomfort, we face it, armed with the knowledge that action provides the antidote. The skier taking action and skiing down the hill relieved the discomfort she felt at the prospect of skiing down an intermediate hill. My daughter's fear of diving was relieved by the act of diving.

As illustrated in figure 4-2, to deny the discomfort only makes it worse. When you take an aspirin to relieve a headache from on-the-job

Figure 4-1:
The Safety/Accountability Cycle

Figure 4-2:
The Pain/Denial Cycle

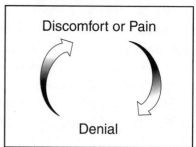

stress, you basically go into denial about the stress. You'll probably end up with stronger headaches down the road unless the underlying stress vanishes as well. And although the headache may go away temporarily, the cycle will continue until extra-strength aspirin no longer dulls the pain. When the body experiences too much pain, it goes into shock, but when your emotions experience too much pain, you go numb. So you no longer feel the stress of the job until you go on vacation and discover five days later what you're really like when you aren't stressed.

In a workplace of constant change and pressure to achieve greater results, people tend to respond either with discomfort and pain, or numbness and denial. And just think: These are people who have been "empowered" to lead for the last ten years. The question now becomes, how do you lead people to greater levels of safety and accountability, so they will be truly empowered to assume the risks of breaking old paradigms?

Denial at Work: A Case Study

A team of project managers was several months late completing their project. They asked me to review their process in order to find the hidden breakdown causing their problem. I asked how their meetings were going. "Our team meetings are great!" claimed the team leader. "We have an agenda; everyone shows up on time and is well prepared for the discussion. We're clear on the outcomes, and everyone participates, sharing ideas openly."

I offered to review their process at the next meeting. Sure enough, the leader was correct on every account. I was most impressed with their openness in discussing the issues that surfaced. However, about a quarter of the way through the meeting, it became clear that *they weren't making any decisions or taking any action.* I stopped the group and expressed my observation, but they insisted they needed to have this discussion before they could make any decisions. Half the meeting went by. I repeated my observation. "No outcomes have been accomplished yet," I said. They insisted that they were on track with regard to their agenda. Finally, at the end of the meeting, I asked the team how they felt about their meeting. "It was a great meeting!" they told me. "We had a great discussion!"

Not only were they in denial, they were slaves to the process of their "perfect meeting." I agreed that they had held a great discussion. But I also reflected the other truth of the situation, which was that they had made no progress on their desired outcomes for the meeting and would need to have the same discussion again at their next meeting.

Aware that they might perceive me as being judgmental, I asked a question to help surface the truth of the situation more clearly. "How often do you have great discussions, but then have to deal with the same issues at the next meeting?"

"Most of the time," they admitted.

"No wonder you are late on your project," I said. "You aren't making decisions or taking the actions necessary for making progress." This left them stunned, feeling the full force of the pain of their denial.

Now they were ready to face their need to change. I told them I had also observed that they had the thinking ability and skills necessary to solve their issues. Reassuring though this may have been, I knew that it did not provide them with enough safety to lead them to action. When people are experiencing the discomfort of the situation, they are often discouraged, confused, and consumed with self-doubt.

Once receptive, I spent the next hour leading them through the process of surfacing issues, making decisions, and agreeing to take action. Based on this demonstration, they were now empowered to carry the process forward to future meetings. As a result, they completed their project in six months—one month ahead of schedule.

Moving from Denial to Accountability

When a group (or individual) is in denial, there are three steps to facilitate taking accountability. As illustrated in figure 4-3, step 1 is to increase accountability when a group is in denial. This is achieved by telling the "truth" about the situation. Once the "truth" of the situation is realized, people will tend to experience the "pain" or discomfort of the situation. Step 2 is to increase safety for the person to experience his discomfort and to prepare for taking action. This is accomplished by acknowledging his discomfort without judging him for being uncomfortable, believing in him, and encouraging him to take action. However, the person may not know what actions to take, given that what he has been doing so far hasn't worked. Step 3 is providing the person in denial with guidance using specific steps for taking action. By taking action, the person builds his own "safety" and self-confidence to continue taking more accountability.

Have the Courage to Tell the Truth

If a nonperformer on your team thinks he is doing a good job, and no one

Figure 4-3:
Moving from Denial to Accountability

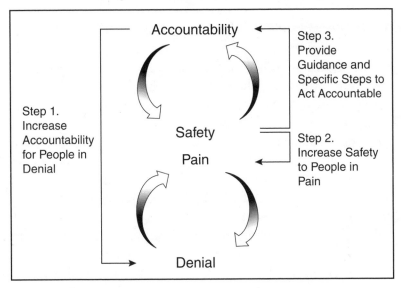

tells him differently, does his performance change? Of course not. Therefore, when someone is in denial, it is important to hold him accountable by reflecting to him the truth of the situation. This truth is not a philosophical truth, but a simple, accurate, and nonjudgmental reflection of the events that are taking place. Any hint of judgment will send that person into a defensive posture, and he'll return to his state of denial.

You tend to withhold the truth because you are afraid of the reaction you may get. The person may feel angry or hurt by your feedback. For you to remain comfortable, you "dance" around the truth in a way that makes your message unclear. Even worse, you don't share the "truth" with the person who is the subject of the comment; you share it with others who will agree with you. Jack Stack summarized the importance of telling the truth in his book, *The Great Game of Business*, when he said, "You only build credibility by telling the truth. You simply can't operate unless people believe you and believe one another."[1]

Of course, whenever you are telling the "truth," it is still only your perception that you are revealing, which is why it is important to refrain from your judgments and opinions as much as possible. It is especially

1. Jack Stack, *The Great Game of Business*, Currency Doubleday, 1991.

important to refrain from telling the "truth" from a self-righteous position.

Don't Remove People's Pain

When you accept the truth relating to your denial, you will feel a level of pain or discomfort. This is not bad news. You often experience your greatest transformations when you are feeling uncomfortable as a result of your current situation. Charles Handy describes this stage of "pain" in his discussion of the "Sigmoid Curve." In essence, every curve goes up and then down. He says, "The secret to constant growth is to start a new curve before the first one peters out."[2] However, when you are moving from one curve to another or from one state to another, there is usually confusion, frustration, and discontentment until you see the new path more clearly.

When people are feeling the "pain" of the truth and the current situation, they may express it in many forms including anger, resistance, hurt, rebellion, or apathy. You must remember that their expression isn't wrong, in need of correction, or a problem to be solved. Holding people accountable when they are in pain or making them comfortable by taking away pain only leads them back into *denial*. Instead, you must provide them with enough *safety* to permit them to feel (rather than deny) their pain. You do this by recognizing that they are uncomfortable or in pain about the situation and then by expressing your belief in them to be successful. I am grateful for the mentors in my life who believed in me when I stopped believing in myself during periods of confusion and self-doubt. It is also important to encourage the person to keep moving and progressing, because it is only through movement and action that you can transition past your fear of the unknown. Figure 4-3, step 2, illustrates that when someone is in pain from experiencing the truth of the situation, it is important to provide the person with safety by offering acceptance, belief, and encouragement. This is very different from making them comfortable by removing the pain.

Stop "Empowering" and Start Guiding

One of the greatest errors in the last few decades is the notion of

2. Charles Handy, *The Age of Paradox*, Harvard Business School Press, 1994.

empowering people whenever you want them to take action. Under the guise of empowerment, you abdicate your role of leadership when you are not providing the necessary guidance for others to be successful. This creates great frustration and discouragement among employees.

When people are experiencing the discomfort of change, you need to provide specific action steps that will guide them through their pain to the point at which they can take action and achieve results. When my daughter was standing at the side of the pool, it wouldn't have worked for me to *empower* her. I needed to *encourage and direct* her into the water so she could gain her own experience and create her own safety to try it again. Figure 4-3, step 3, illustrates the need to provide guidance and specific action steps to assist people from moving to accountability from a place of safety.

The following pattern is sadly familiar to many of us. Management reflects the truth of a bad situation and announces a change to respond to the bad situation. People respond with resistance. Recognizing people's discomfort, management revises its story of the truth by dismissing it, "it wasn't as bad as we thought." Then, they either slow down or stop the change. Within a few months, the change can no longer be avoided, and now, because of waiting, the bad situation is worse. Then management forces the change on people by "empowering" them to make it on their own (or else face serious consequences). Now people feel completely abandoned by management. They decide that management has no credibility, and they take on a cynical perspective to avoid further disappointment.

This is what happened at a major communications company in California, which announced one September that 30 percent of a 500-person department was going to be downsized in three months. I was called in to help the management team (which was also going to be cut 30 percent) develop a strategy for restructuring the process. Not surprisingly, people expressed plenty of grief.

Once we moved past the anger, we created an implementation plan everyone agreed to. The team made progress on the plan for eight weeks, at which point I went back for a follow-up session. People entered the room even angrier than before. I couldn't understand why, because I knew that they had made steady progress on their plan. It turned out that management had reversed the decision to downsize, claiming that they had acted too hastily. However, management also said that this wouldn't prevent them from downsizing the following year.

It is critical for managers and employees alike to start reflecting the truth, provide encouragement when others are feeling overwhelmed and doubtful, and more important, provide guidance in the form of *specific action to move through the change.*

Conclusion: Ten Ways to Create Safe Accountability in Your Organization

1. *Set clear and mutually agreed upon expectations* with people with regard to both performance and behavior. This reduces confusion, mixed messages, and judgments of nonperformance.

2. *Share information* openly and at appropriate times to avoid unnecessary surprises.

3. *Surface any conflict directly* with the person involved. Focus on ways to avoid conflict in the future. (This is far more effective than avoiding the person, telling everyone else about the conflict, or blaming the person as the one who was wrong.)

4. *Provide encouragement, guidance, and other forms of support* to individuals who need to make a change but who may not realize the importance, or the process, of doing so. Typically, we either ignore people struggling because we're too busy, or we sympathize with their discomfort and let them off the hook.

5. *Focus on functional roles and processes*, rather than position and power, to accomplish outcomes.

6. *Support the development of people and systems* to respond to the needs of tomorrow and to avoid reacting only to crises.

7. *Monitor and measure the results* of each team and individual so that people know exactly where they stand. This is the only way to make people aware of their successes and their need for improvement.

8. *Do not allow people to perform or behave poorly* without making it clear that their performance or behavior is unacceptable. Skirting the issue only causes people to feel deceived and victimized. No one benefits from carrying a poor performer. The organization loses, the team loses, and so does the individual.

9. *Follow up on commitments* so that people can depend on your words and your consistency. If you are unable to keep a commitment, let people know as soon as you know.

10. *Let others know the care, appreciation, and compassion you feel,* instead of holding back. Honor their humanity as well as your own. When all is said and done, we are FIRST human beings with fears, needs, and imperfections, and SECOND employees hired to complete a job.

CHAPTER 5

LEADERSHIP ROLES THAT PRODUCE BREAKTHROUGH RESULTS

MYTH: Senior management must act accountably before the organization can be accountable.

TRUTH: Middle management must act accountably as a unified team before the organization can be accountable.

I GREW UP BELIEVING THAT TEACHERS TAUGHT and students learned. The roles were clear, and leadership was a singular role held by the teacher. Although this approach to education was changing by the time I became a teacher, it was still clear that my responsibility was to lead the educational experience for students. One year, I taught a high school general math class comprised of sixteen- and seventeen-year-olds who had difficulty with simple arithmetic. Adding, subtracting, multiplying, and dividing were painful processes for these students, even though they were old enough to drive and were approaching voting age.

Peggy, a particularly cooperative student in the class, began to experience some breakthroughs in completing the math assignments, so I introduced her to basic algebra. She understood the concepts, could complete the homework assignments, and was progressing well. Then a wonderful accident occurred that changed my perspective about teaching forever.

I was busy helping a group of students who were having difficulty adding and subtracting fractions. Another student, John, was doing well and interrupted me to ask if I could help him progress to his next level. Because I was busy with the group of students having difficulties, I asked Peggy if she would assist John. Later, when I had a break, I checked to see how John was getting along. To my surprise, he was doing far better than I would have expected. Peggy had turned out to be an excellent teacher. I continued this model of "chain teaching" as students progressed to higher levels of math. By the end of the year, nine students were doing algebra. All had taught someone else at some point through this process of "students as teachers." Until then, students in general math classes had been categorized as unable to handle algebra. Now, they were not only able to learn algebra, they were also teaching it!

> Yet successful organizations have leaders at *all* levels of the organization.

A similar strategy can be used in the workplace. Typically, we assume that leadership is the exclusive domain of *management*. Yet successful organizations have leaders at *all* levels of the organization. Although each person's leadership role is different, it is critical to have leaders who will direct people toward a unified focus, implement changes to achieve the impossible, develop others in the organization, and bring new skills and expertise to the organization. Regardless of whether people are in management or nonmanagement positions, there will be leadership roles for them.

When an organization isn't accomplishing its desired outcomes, the tendency is for employees to blame supervisors, for middle managers to blame upper managers, and for upper managers to blame employees. When people are blaming each other for the problems that exist, it is a sign that they are not assuming a leadership role to solve those problems. The notion that leadership is reserved for people in management denies the responsibility that each person has to take charge of and be accountable for his or her performance and relationship with others. When an organization is committed to accountability, leadership roles exist at all levels. People are accountable for moving themselves *and* their team to the next level of performance within the parameters of their respective roles.

Stop Waiting for Executives to Change

Because executives are responsible for steering the "organizational ship," middle managers and others in the organization play a "waiting game" in regard to executives. They give up their power waiting for executives to change before taking action to make things better.

A group of middle managers participated in a leadership development program. They were given the opportunity to create their own vision of leadership and improvement goals for increasing the organization's effectiveness. At first, they refused to do the assignment, claiming it was the executive's role, not theirs. Fortunately, one manager in the group challenged that premise and inspired the others to take initiative and not wait for direction from executives.

Based on completing their assignment, the group became a team; together, they implemented the changes that they agreed on. Six months later, they were given more leadership authority and responsibility by the executive team.

When you take the position of waiting for another group to be accountable before you become accountable, you are automatically in a "victim" cycle. You are waiting for the *external* environment to change before *you* change, and this means you are giving up your power and influence. Executives have become a great scapegoat for the lack of change and movement of an organization, but there is a lot that middle management and others can do to initiate change and create breakthrough results.

The roles for each level within an organization is determined by the "direct" accountability required for achieving results and linking with other levels or functions to achieve results. Confusion regarding roles contribute to the "blame game" and to a general lack of accountability. Accordingly, executives are "catalysts" for achieving results, middle managers are "change agents," and employees are "customer activists." Let's look at each of these levels and roles in detail.

Executives are Catalysts for Achieving Results, *Not* Change Agents

A CEO of a national journal was faced with a declining market. Besides having to create a new look for his publication, he had to change the focus of its content in order to appeal to a wider audience. At staff meetings, employees would grumble about the journal's lack of direction. "We should be focused more on the environment," claimed one employee.

"I think spirituality should be our major purpose," said another. Someone else claimed that the journal should stick to its roots and continue running articles on traditional research from leading studies on psychology.

They all expressed their views with much conviction, and these views reflected their own interests and those of their colleagues who had similar interests. However, none of the staff were accountable for the results of their opinions in terms of ensuring customer acceptance and profitability. The organization remained fragmented for several months while staff members continued to present their opinions at meetings on this subject. At last the CEO took a different approach to determine the journal's direction.

The CEO determined the "ideal" customer base by age and interest in order to provide the largest readership possible. Then he had a market research company survey those readers for their specific interests and issues. The acquired information provided the basis for a clear direction of focus for the journal. Based on customer interests, the CEO clearly explained the new direction of the journal and was able to win support from most of the staff, even though most of them had earlier made very different suggestions. Within a few weeks, the organization demonstrated unity, focus, and alignment, and readership improved within the next several months.

Coming out of graduate school, I was conditioned to think that change had to begin with top management. This translated to the expectation that executives had to change before anyone else could. Although I have seen some executive teams become accountable, few have sufficiently adopted the very changes which they promoted. Because their role is strategic and *not* operational, they generally can't demonstrate the changes they are promoting without also micromanaging. Their role is to provide direction and be a catalyst for change, not necessarily modeling the change in a way that others would expect. Unfortunately, managers and employees use this as an excuse to resist becoming more accountable. *Executives are not the change agents.*

Instead, executives are the *catalysts* for achieving results and setting the tone for the culture. As such, their role is to *articulate the direction and desired outcomes* in a clear and unified front to establish the path for movement and progress. If executives aren't clear about the desired outcomes and priorities, then the organization will become paralyzed in confusion. Their communication must be strategically delivered to create the greatest level of focus and action (as detailed in chapter 11).

Executives: Have the Courage to Set a Clear Direction
One of the most frequent complaints I hear throughout an organization concerns "lack of direction." Mission statements full of rhetoric, "flavor-of-the-month" change efforts, and a multitude of (often-conflicting) priorities bombard people. Without clear direction, managers can't effectively prioritize workloads or make good decisions, and paralysis results. Executives must stop avoiding their true accountability and take a stand on the future direction of the organization.

The future direction is determined by the "external drivers" to which the organization must respond. These are conditions that the organization can't change and, therefore, must respond to in order to stay viable. I refer to external drivers as "non-negotiables." They include factors such as:

- Changes in customer expectations
- Technology advancements
- Societal needs
- Competitive trends
- Government regulation and intervention
- Trends in supplier markets
- Financial constraints
- Market trends

Executives have more direct access to the organization's external drivers than anyone else in the organization. Because they aren't managing daily operations, they can serve on government committees that impact legislation affecting the organization. They can participate in community groups that represent the societal trends in the customer base (as opposed to the needs of individual customers which are best represented by employees). And they can analyze the other external drivers that impact the organization, including market studies, economic changes, financial trends, technological advances, and so on. Whereas all other levels of the organization are responsible for ensuring the daily performance that serves current customers, executives have access to the external drivers that continue to prepare and shape the organization for the future.

Therefore, the primary responsibility of executives is to establish *a clear direction* for the future of the organization as well as *clear financial, cultural, operational, and related parameters* for creating that future. Although they may gather input from others, it is not acceptable for executives to delegate the decision of the organization's direction to a committee. Ultimately, they are the ones responsible for producing a *strategic business plan* that clearly articulates the business outcomes and priorities necessary for the organization to thrive over the next few years.

It is also their responsibility to identify the type of *culture* necessary for achieving those business outcomes in the most effective manner. Identifying the ideal culture is not just a question of ethics or values, but also one of performance execution to achieve business outcomes. At the heart of this direction is the determination of whether the organization will function at a level 2 (individual), 3 (work unit), or 4 (cross-functional) on the accountability continuum (see figure 1-1 on page 5).

Part of this role includes communicating a clear message about the desired outcome and priorities, as well as providing the understanding, background, and context for necessary changes. As will be described in chapter 6, this includes creating an "intention" about the future—a detailed vision that consists of:

- The mission for the organization

- The values representing the culture of the organization

- The response to those external drivers that direct the organization's future

The desired business outcomes and direction of the organization may evolve in a fast-paced and changing business environment, which is why executives must be accountable for setting priorities with regard to them. With continuous changes being forged by the external drivers, executives must update and clarify the priorities on a regular basis. Otherwise, people continue to add to their list of priorities, and they become fragmented and overwhelmed. As a result, they fail to achieve the expected business results necessary to make progress. All executives must continually restate the desired outcomes and articulate the priorities of the organization as the emphasis shifts.

Because executives are responsible for the direction of the organization, they are also accountable for ensuring that the organization stays on track. Although they aren't responsible for taking specific actions, they are responsible for *monitoring the progress* made to achieve the organization's priorities and direction. This includes both *performance-oriented priorities* as well as *cultural changes* directly associated with achieving the organization's desired business outcomes.

Executives are also accountable for *identifying and communicating the consequences* of failing to achieve the organization's desired business outcomes. These must be presented not as a threat of punishment, but as an honest reflection of the reality of the impact such failures will have on the organization's viability. Finally, executives must *guide and coach* middle managers on their strategy of operational change based on the desired business outcomes. This does not mean that executives are expected to solve tactical operational problems; only that they must guide the strategy for overcoming global organizational challenges that prevent progress. For example, this may involve finding ways to use the organization's resources more effectively by setting up cross-functional operations systems. Finally, executives need to ensure that the linkages and functioning between all levels of the organization are maintained properly by middle managers.

The Plight of Middle Management

Danny, one of my closest childhood friends, was the first born in a family of three children. As the oldest, Danny was clearly the leader of his younger sister and brother. Because I was an only child, I was interested in observing him and his siblings interact. One day, Danny's parents asked him to take care of his younger brother and sister while they went out to buy groceries for dinner. "Don't let them get into any trouble while we're gone," said his dad.

Danny did his best to live up to his parents' expectations. At the same time, he also wanted to play with his brother and sister. Of course, as soon as he took on the role of protector and leader, his siblings banded together, leaving him out. Soon a fight broke out between the two younger children. Danny stepped in as the boss, which only fueled the fight because his brother and sister were not about to cooperate with his new position of authority. By the time his parents returned, they were all yelling and screaming at each other. Danny's father turned to him, furious, and demanded, "What happened? Can't we leave you in charge for even a half-hour without World War III breaking out?" Danny was sent to his room, and his brother and sister were sent outside to play.

When I talk with middle managers and supervisors, they make me think of Danny. They're caught in the middle, desperately trying to serve executives who "don't understand," while the employees are fighting among themselves, not cooperating, and blaming middle management for the problems.

Because executives are not directly involved with day-to-day operations, they are not well positioned to control operational improvements without also micromanaging. Middle management, on the other hand, is ideally positioned to do so. Executives who insist on being the ones to control operational processes end up becoming roadblocks. In such circumstances, middle managers and employees will make recommendations for improvement, and these will go to the executive team for approval, where they will sit for months waiting for executives to make a decision. The reality is that, although executives can make decisions as to the *global direction* of the organization, they are too far removed to make decisions regarding the *day-to-day operations*. Unfortunately, many executive teams are afraid to hand over that control to middle managers.

Actually, there is good reason for their reluctance. Middle managers are only accountable for the performance of their department. They are structured as isolated islands within an organization. Some call these departments "silos." Although virtually every department has a major impact on the success of every other department, conflicting priorities and the desire to make one's own department look best create territorialism that dominates most organizations. Middle managers feel disempowered, because as individuals, they don't have the authority to make meaningful decisions that will impact the way the organization functions. This creates the barriers most bitterly discussed among employees. An executive for a leading insurance company said it well: "Middle managers are personally accountable in our organization. When a problem surfaces that impacts several middle managers, each one works hard to solve the problems in their department. However, we are good at solving problems, we just aren't 'fixing' them. Not one of our managers takes initiative as a steward for the organization to bring all of the middle managers together with the purpose of fixing the problem. So, we are constantly fighting fires and solving problems that continually recur."

> Middle managers must become accountable not only for their own departments but also for the operational effectiveness of the entire organization.

Ironically, middle managers are positioned to serve as the ideal cross-functional team in the organization, because they represent the operations of every major department. Although their job should be to make the operational decisions as a cross-functional team that will lead the organization to achieving its desired business outcomes, they instead generally get bogged down in territorial infighting over position, power, and resources. As a result, the improvements recommended by middle managers tend to be shortsighted at best, causing middle managers to lose respect in the eyes of executives and employees. Over time, they become *caretakers* rather than *initiators of improvement.*

For an organization to optimize its performance and to quickly respond to the demands of its customers and external environment, the role of middle management must change. Middle managers must become accountable not only for their own departments but also for the operational effectiveness of the entire organization. Janet Lowe presents the views of Jack Welch in her book *Jack Welch Speaks*, where

Welch is quoted as saying, "Boundaryless behavior laughs at the concept of little kingdoms called finance, engineering, manufacturing, and marketing, sending each other specs and memos, and instead gets them all together in a room to wrestle with issues as a team."[1]

The reality described here demands an entirely different mind-set as to the structure and role of middle management.

Middle Managers: From Territorial Tycoons to a Team of Change Agents

Revolutionaries in history attacked the "establishment" on the basis of a "cause." In the United States, the English redcoats represented the "establishment" and the "cause" was democracy. In organizations, the "establishment" is represented by antiquated methods of leadership along with dysfunctional operational habits. The "cause" is achieving breakthrough results in half the time expected. The revolutionaries are middle managers dedicated as a team of "change agents" to eliminate dysfunctional processes and habits that undermine successful achievement of desired outcomes.

Although a *strategic business plan* developed by executives outlines the specific direction of the organization, a *strategic operations plan* is what translates that direction into action. Therefore, middle managers, who oversee and control operations, are in the best position to develop and manage an organization's strategic operations plan. This can be accomplished only when each manager has a full understanding of the impact that each department has on the other departments. The operational strategy, utilization of resources, and priorities must be linked and integrated in order to ensure a unified, coordinated, and aligned focus and effort. Otherwise, operational fragmentation pulls apart the organization and causes it to spin its wheels.

To achieve this level of effectiveness, middle managers must be formed into a cross-functional team where they develop a clear vision of leadership for which they all become accountable. This should include their commitment to ensuring the operational success of the organization as a higher priority than the success of their own individual

1. Janet Lowe, *Jack Welch Speaks: Wisdom from the World's Greatest Business Leader,* John Wiley & Sons, Inc., 1998.

---

department. Tom Peters describes this well in his book, *Thriving on Chaos*, where he notes that "Middle managers are to be responsible for seeking out and battering down the very functional barriers that they were formerly paid to protect. They are to be charged with making things happen, come hell or high water."[2]

The vision of leadership is always futuristic and, as such, involves a "stretch" beyond the current situation. Specifically, it includes:

- A description of the reputation that leaders want to have with employees

- The teamwork necessary to achieve that reputation

- The role of leaders in ensuring organizational viability and success

All of these dimensions are included in the statement of intention developed by the leadership team.

Grounded in this commitment and in the practice of sharing information and resources, middle management develops a strategic operations plan to accomplish the priorities of the executive team's strategic business plan. As a team, middle managers identify the priorities of the operation. They identify the dysfunctional habits that require change, the strategy for making those changes, and the tracking system to ensure transformation of the culture. This includes aspects of the organization's functioning as demonstrated by performance management systems, strategic communication systems, recognition systems, decision-making processes, and processes for resolving conflicts. Middle management functions as a team that:

- *Makes operational decisions* with global and cross-functional ramifications

- *Takes action* by developing new habits to replace dysfunctional ones

- *Resolves conflicts* or problems that block employee success

2. Tom Peters, *Thriving on Chaos: Handbook for a Management Revolution*, Harper Perennial, 1987.

In an accountable organization, middle managers also become accountable to one another. Each department performs in accordance with an agreed-upon operational strategic plan that is created and monitored by the middle management team.

The role of middle management, then, becomes twofold:

1. *Middle managers are responsible for organizational success.* This includes cross-functional operations, the culture that ensures effective functioning and linkage between departments, and the monitoring of organizational performance to ensure that business outcomes are being achieved.

2. *Middle managers are responsible for department success.* This includes the performance of their respective departments and for eliminating dysfunctional habits in their department that prevents departmental and organizational success.

Middle Managers in Action: A Case Study

A highly complex and technically based electronics firm had experienced several years of declining revenue and profits. Senior management made the decision to expand into new market segments that would grow the business and ensure future viability. Although this new strategic business direction was on track for developing new business, the organization wasn't *operationally* prepared to meet the needs of this new business. Set up in the normal hierarchy, with department managers responsible for the performance of their respective departments, the organization continued to fail to meet its revenue goals and performance objectives.

At first, senior management complained that the department managers weren't being accountable enough for the performance of their departments. They would have monthly sessions to review each manager's department and then blame the managers for not meeting the objectives. On the surface, the blame seemed justified. However, upon closer examination, it became evident that the root of the problem lay elsewhere.

Although the managers were being held accountable for the performance of their respective departments, no culture existed in the organization for removing nonperformers. No individual manager was in a position to begin to deal with nonperformance because there was no norm established for doing so. We discovered a basic lack of skill in project management throughout the organization. However, because each middle manager operated within individual silos, they had no idea that it was a systemic problem that could be resolved. Finally, there were conflicting priorities, functional breakdowns, and a lack of coordination among departments that never got surfaced or addressed because the managers spent all of their time in their respective departments trying to manage crises and defend poor performance.

We formed a middle management team and gave them the expanded role of *changing the culture* with cross-functional processes to improve overall performance. Immediately, the organizational breakdowns surfaced and were resolved. Middle managers developed a strategy for identifying and dealing with nonperformers by either coaching them into good performance or assisting them out of the organization through corrective action. Because all managers were doing this together, the change was easier to make. In addition, middle managers established a program to develop all project managers in a consistent manner to support better performance. The conflicts that existed among departments were prioritized by the middle management team and resolved by subcommittees that reported back to the team.

As a result, performance improved significantly within the first six months of change, middle managers were now leading the global operational changes, and all levels of the organization felt a greater sense of cohesiveness and focus on the priorities driving their organizational success.

Individual Accountability:
The Heart of an Accountable Organization

"It's not my job."

"No one told me to do that."

"It's the other department's fault."

Sound familiar? As long as others are busy expressing their defensiveness, frustration, and resistance, we can't complete our jobs, customers aren't having their needs met, and the organization is unable to make the changes needed to stay competitive.

When we can't count on each other, everyone loses. Regardless of position or function, we must be able to count on each other if we are to succeed.

Accountability involves *each individual in the organization* regardless of position or function. We all must keep our commitments to perform, our agreements to sustain effective team relationships, and our level of effort given to support others when support is requested or required. In virtually all high-performing teams, teammates help each other out. We see this with music groups learning a difficult piece, soccer teams improving the execution of their passing game, theatrical groups memorizing the lines of a production, and military units covering for one another in battle. It's this level of accountability that each person demonstrates on a day-to-day basis that builds the morale and the pride of an organization. The confidence that we can count on each other during the rough times is what helps get us through those rough times.

But first, you have to be able to count on yourself to keep your own commitments. Being accountable depends on *your* ability, willingness, courage, and commitment to renew your attitudes and behaviors in order to achieve your desired outcomes. This formula for *personal accountability* doesn't just apply to the workplace. We also have desired outcomes or goals related to our families, careers, personal growth, and communities. If we become aware of an area in which we are failing to meet our desired outcomes, then we have to ask ourselves, "Do I have the *ability*?" Usually, our ability reflects what we thought was required. For instance, as described in chapter 3, the ability of many people to use a typewriter became obsolete once word processing was introduced. Whether we are talking about our ability to parent well as our children grow older, or our ability to perform well on the job with changing technology, we must continue to upgrade our ability to meet the demands of the future. You probably know people who have reached a plateau with regard to their skills. They think that they have completed learning, growing, and evolving.

It's acceptable to find ourselves unable to achieve our desired outcomes so long as we have the *willingness to* seek the training, coaching, mentoring, or counseling required to gain the ability. In some cases, we can't develop the skills fast enough, and so we may need to call on others in our sphere of influence (such as coworkers and family members) as resources to help us in achieving our desired outcomes.

Unfortunately, territorialism in the workplace might prevent us from drawing on someone else's skills to get the job done.

If we lack the willingness to call on others, it is usually due to our ego and pride, which can become a serious roadblock to the achievement of our desired outcomes. It is amazing (yet human) to sabotage our own best interests simply because we have difficulty admitting weaknesses or mistakes.

It takes *courage* to look in the mirror of personal observation to check out our flaws. It takes commitment to *do* something about them by changing our attitudes and behaviors. David McNally speaks of the importance of commitment in his book, *Even Eagles Need a Push*: "Commitment is the willingness to do whatever it takes to get what you want. A true commitment is a heartfelt promise to yourself from which you will not back down. Many people have dreams and many have good intentions, but few are willing to make the commitment necessary for their attainment."[3]

Everyone knows people who have been blessed with plenty of talent but who have an unfortunate attitude of self-righteousness or arrogance that prevents them from achieving their goals.

Increasing your level of accountability is explained in detail in the book, *The Power of Personal Accountability: Achieve What Matters to You.*

Success Can Be Our Biggest Obstacle

We all want to be successful. But once we demonstrate some measure of success, we must beware of the trap of thinking that "we have arrived, we have made it, we can rest now." Success is a *process*, not an *event*. Whether you are the president of a corporation who assumes that because your organization has 60 percent of the market, it is the secured leader in the industry, or whether you are a senior manager who thinks that your position makes your job secure, you are laboring under the "success illusion."

You've heard stories about entrepreneurs who go belly up after experiencing great financial success, or straight "A" high school students who later drop out of college because they can't make the grade or because getting "Cs" was unacceptable to them. Attaining success is not nearly as important as sustaining success. You can sustain success only by responding to the many changes that affect your life, whether they be changes in technology, changes in customer needs, changes in organizational constraints (such as resources), or changes in competition. On the personal level, these include changes in your physical health,

3. David McNally, *Even Eagles Need a Push: Learning to Soar in a Changing World*, Dell Publishing, 1990.

your family relationships, your friendships, and your financial changes. You must continually adapt your skills, attitude, and behaviors. Otherwise, you wake up one day to find that you have lost your position, your money, or your relationships—and didn't even see it coming.

Employees: From Whiners and Blamers to Customer Activists

Leaders can lead and managers can manage, but, without employees, customers aren't served, processes aren't improved, new leaders aren't developed, and organizations can't survive. Each employee, regardless of position or title, has a leadership role in contributing to the evolution of an organization. Employees must be activists for change, not only for the sake of the organization, but also for their own sakes. How do you become an effective customer activist?

1. *You must first be service-oriented.* The rising popularity of customer service over the past decade has been a great first step, but, as most of us have discovered, we are all "customers" to one another. Being service-oriented is not just about meeting the needs of others; it is also about having the right attitude of helpfulness, assistance, coaching, and support. It means replacing the ego-oriented position on which you base your agenda with doing whatever is necessary to get the job done in a manner that supports success for yourself and for those around you.

2. *You must dedicate yourself to being the best you can be.* Whether you are a manager, a computer programmer, or a clerical administrator, you must look for opportunities to streamline your processes, improve your linkages with those who depend on you, and develop your skills to continue performing at higher levels of excellence. This might mean becoming involved on committees to improve performance or make changes, or offering suggestions to coworkers and upper management regarding how to improve services, or even cooperating with changes that you don't necessarily like. It also means continually learning, practicing, and expanding your skills in order to develop greater confidence in the knowledge that you can

handle the unusual and challenging situations that continuously arise. Just like top athletes, musicians, and dancers, you will continue to hone your skills.

3. *You must dedicate yourself to supporting others,* especially those whose work will have an impact on and be affected by you. You must make an effort to understand their needs and constraints. This is critical for effective coordination, cooperation, and sharing of information. You cannot be successful without the support of others, and you must foster that support to be an effective customer activist.

4. *You must continue to learn new skills outside of your specialty* so that you can adapt to the changes that you can't control. You can achieve this through cross-training with others on your teams, and taking advantage of workshops and other learning opportunities. Investing in your growth and development in order to increase your awareness and overcome any of your own attitudinal or behavioral blocks will lead to higher levels of success. As the amount of change you face continues to increase exponentially, your ability to anticipate those changes becomes even more difficult, and so it is critical for you to continue to "stretch yourself" in order to maintain and further develop your flexibility and adaptability.

5. *You must keep your eye on the future and on external drivers,* anticipating changes in your customers, changes in technology, changes in your organization, changes in your personal needs, and any other changes in society that may have an impact on your job, your profession, or your career. This is a new skill that every employee should be developing by reading the newspaper and trade journals, talking to upper management, and attending meetings with industry specialists.

An organization made up of customer activists like those described here will be able to anticipate future needs, respond to those needs, and sustain high levels of performance through the involvement and growth of its workforce. However, the benefits extend beyond the organization. Customer activists themselves benefit by acquiring greater self-confidence, greater flexibility, and more nurturing and satisfying relationships with others.

Conclusion: Success Happens When Everyone Works Together

Success is more easily sustained when each level of an organization assumes accountability for its distinct role. Here's a recap for each group:

1. *Senior managers* (catalysts for results and change) should lead and guide the organizational direction and the culture in response to external drivers.

2. *Middle managers* (change agents) should guide the culture and operations to ensure effective linkages and the removal of unnecessary obstacles.

3. *Employees* (customer activists) should be dedicated to improving their relationships with others and their performance as it impacts the customer as well as the organization.

Figure 5-1 describes in detail what each of these three groups should do to bring about an accountable organization.

Ultimately, it is each person's responsibility at every position in the organization to be dedicated to his or her own growth and improvement as well as the support of others improving in the organization. In his book *The Fifth Discipline*, Peter Senge highlights the importance of self-improvement by noting: "At the heart of a learning organization is a shift of mind from seeing ourselves as separate from the world to connected to the world, from seeing problems as caused by someone and something 'out there' to seeing how our own actions create problems we experience."[4]

Ultimately, your goal is to be accountable for your own actions and dedicated to your own improvement so that you can achieve your desired outcomes. With an accountable environment in place, the organization is able to recover quickly—through focus, involvement, and dedication at all levels—from any dips in success that may occur.

4. Peter Senge, *The Fifth Discipline*, Currency Doubleday, 1990.

Figure 5-1: Leadership Roles that Produce Breakthrough Results	
Levels	**Roles of Leadership**
Senior managers are "catalysts for results and change."	Translate external drivers into a clear strategic business plan. Monitor and guide middle management in achieving operational priorities, improvement projects, and operational performance consistent with achieving the outcomes of the strategic business plan.
Middle managers are "change agents."	Translate the strategic business plan into a strategic operations plan. Align efforts around the operational priorities, strategize and monitor operational priorities, effectively share resources, and develop project plans to achieve the strategic operational plan. Improve the operational infrastructure to remove obstacles and to support employees in performing to satisfy their customers. Assure effective and strategic communications to mobilize the workforce and to develop future leaders according to the changing needs of the organization.
Employees are "customer activists."	Identify and meet customer expectations. Improve technical processes and individual performance to meet operational priorities established by the strategic operational plan and the changing cultural environment.

PART TWO

SIX STRATEGIES FOR LEADING WITH ACCOUNTABILITY

Strategy #1:
From Empty Platitudes to Clear Direction

Strategy #2:
Translating Clear Direction into Non-Negotiable Priorities

Strategy #3:
Execution: The Key to High Performance

Strategy #4:
Proactive Recovery: The Secret to Accountable
Performance Execution

Strategy #5:
Create a Plan for Change that Guarantees Results

Strategy #6:
Communicate to Influence "Non-Believers"

Get Started: Your Next Steps to Get Breakthrough Results

CHAPTER 6

STRATEGY #1:
FROM EMPTY PLATITUDES
TO CLEAR DIRECTION

MYTH: Creating inspiring platitudes establishes clear direction.

TRUTH: Creating a clear picture of success is necessary for establishing a clear direction.

VISION STATEMENTS TEND TO LOOK MORE LIKE MARKETING MATERIAL than statements of direction. Scratch the surface of a vision statement, and you're likely to find yourself poking through to a hollow core, like one of those chocolate Easter bunnies. "Our organization is world class," or "we strive to be better than the best." Perhaps this can look good in a marketing brochure and can even inspire employees for a short period of time. However, it isn't long before the statement becomes another trite and ineffective way to motivate people using empty words.

The purpose of an effective vision statement is to provide a clear and meaningful direction, inspiring people to attain a new level of excellence. A vision statement represents the intention of the organization, department, or team based on the aspirations, values, and clear sense of purpose of the authors. The statement isn't necessarily to be memorized, but it provides a clear picture that people can become a part of as they read it. When a vision is clear, it reads like an action-oriented story that provides clear accountability, expectation, and outcomes that could be measured. *The Power of Personal Accountability* dedicates a complete chapter on this topic called, "Take Charge of Your Life." The vision statement in this chapter is referred to as your "intention."

Translate Words into Actions

Max DePree makes this point in his inspiring book on leadership, *Leadership Jazz:* "Accountable for 'what' and 'to whom'? . . . are precisely the kinds of questions that so many boards of directors and boards of trustees should be asking themselves. I imagine that quite a few stockholders and faculty members and students would like to hear the answers."[1]

Integrate Outcomes, Values, and External Drivers

Have you ever seen a vintage water faucet with two spouts, one for hot and one for cold? These faucets worked well when you either wanted hot water or cold water. Because they were separate, it was challenging when you wanted warm water. The same is true when you keep your business outcomes, your mission, and your values separate. Fragmentation and separation occur, instead of a blending and integration, which gives meaning to all three. As a result, confusion sets in, direction is unclear, or only the priority of the moment gets acted upon—business outcomes, mission, or values, but not all three.

The ability to define and articulate a clear business outcome and direction depends on three elements, all involving understanding:

1. *A clear understanding of the organization's mission in terms of the desired impact on its customers along with the return on investment necessary to be financially viable.* Most organizations invest time creating a clear mission statement, but they fall into the trap of thinking that it provides sufficient information to establish an understandable sense of direction. The mission only provides *a sense of purpose* for the organization. It doesn't reflect the *style or approach* in which the organization will set about to *accomplish* its purpose.

1. Max DePree, *Leadership Jazz*, Dell Publishing, 1992.

---

2. *A clear understanding of the organization's values.* The values of more evolved organizations are clarified with a *value statement* that details a consistent set of behaviors intended to guide the culture. Understanding what behaviors are consistent with the organization's values helps clarify its direction. Combining the mission of an organization with its values gives a clearer sense of what it means to accomplish the organization's purpose.

3. *A clear understanding and response to the "external drivers" affecting the organization.* Although the mission and values are important, they do not provide employees with a clear sense of direction for how their actions will contribute to the future life of the organization. Without clarifying external drivers that provide the context for change, employees more often move into resistance rather than cooperation. They have no sense of how they fit into the organization's future plans. (We will discuss this further in chapter 7.)

These three elements (mission, values, and response to external drivers) are all required to develop a clear sense of the organization's direction and business outcomes. The mission relates more to performance, the values relate to the culture that creates the performance, and the external drivers relate to the changes in performance and culture necessary to stay viable. To isolate one element from the others results in a less-than-complete picture. They must be entirely integrated. But too often, they are addressed in isolation.

Robert Kaplan and David Norton explain this necessary integration in their book, *The Balanced Scorecard: Translating Strategy into Action.* They developed a process that focuses on four aspects of performance:[2]

1. The financial perspective

2. The customer perspective

3. The internal perspective

4. The internal business perspective

2. Robert S. Kaplan and David P. Norton, *The Balanced Scorecard: Translating Strategy into Action,* Harvard Business School Press, 1996.

This approach would be enhanced by including other external drivers in addition to customers.

It is clear that if we are going to create a new "balanced scorecard," we must identify all the aspects of business that impact the organization. Richard Barrett has done an excellent job of creating a more comprehensive scorecard. In his book, *Liberating the Corporate Soul*, he has expanded the original balanced scorecard to create a "balanced needs scorecard," which includes six areas:[3]

1. Corporate survival

2. Client/supplier relations

3. Corporate culture

4. Society community contribution

5. Corporate evolution

6. Corporate fitness

One common mistake is to treat values independently of mission. Undoubtedly, you can think of at least one organization that has created an entire training and development program that focused the organization on its values, while failing to link those values to the organization's business outcomes (as represented by its mission).

3. Richard Barrett, *Liberating the Corporate Soul: Building a Visionary Organization*, Butterworth-Heinemann, 1998.

Success Through Integration: A Case Study

A senior management team of a federal governmental agency in Baltimore needed to accomplish two important business outcomes and felt that their lack of teamwork was a major obstacle to their success. Several consultants had already tried to build the team's working relationship over the previous two years. They had focused on creating more trust, support, cooperation, and team decision making. By the time I was called in, the team was deeply frustrated with the lack of progress.

I knew that the values of teamwork could not be treated separately from business outcomes, so we set up their team system to accomplish their business outcomes, while integrating the values of teamwork as they had previously defined them. By the end of six months, they had accomplished their two priority projects. Not only that, their levels of trust, communication, decision making, and cooperation had also improved. In fact, the change was so significant that their employees were also beginning to function with a higher level of teamwork based on the modeling of this senior management team.

The leader of the team was amazed. "For two years, we made teamwork our primary focus and didn't accomplish a thing!" he said. "But after making our business outcomes the primary focus and using teamwork as our means, we were able to see the greatest improvements we have ever made."

Creating a Clear Vision Statement

An excellent article by James C. Collins and Jerry I. Porras in the *Harvard Business Review* offers valuable insights into how to build your company's vision: "Vision provides guidance about what to preserve and what to change." It details "a new prescriptive framework" which "adds clarity and rigor to the vague and fuzzy vision concepts at large today."[4] The vision represents an agreed-upon "stretch" to which the organization, department, or team will grow into.

The scope of a vision statement provides a clear intention for excellence beyond what has been previously achieved. It not only describes what *the organization* will be achieving in terms of business objectives; it also addresses how *its customers* will view the organization. It defines the kind of environment in which the organization will operate. And most important, it describes how the organization will function to achieve business outcomes and customer outcomes, and to be responsive to change as change intensifies.

A vision statement needs substance. It must be stated so vividly as to be almost tangible. It is as thorough as any investigative reporter probing into the who, what, where, when, why, and how of company direction.

A vision statement is characterized by four essential elements—it should be:

1. *Responsive.* It identifies the external drivers affecting the organization and how the organization needs to change in order to meet these challenges.

4. James C. Collins and Jerry I. Porras, "Building Your Company's Vision," *Harvard Business Review*, September 1, 1996.

2. *Customer-driven.* It focuses on the organization's distinctiveness and how it wants to be perceived by its customers. It identifies the qualities for which the organization will be known.

3. *Action-oriented.* It defines the internal environment that is required for the vision to become a reality. It includes aspects of performance execution that will need further definition.

4. *Practical.* It describes the contribution to the financial and long-term viability of the organization, its stockholders, and the community at large

Unlike the concept of the balanced scorecard, a vision statement describes the extremes of excellence and leaves open the possibility for paradox. For example, a company can have an intention for high quality and low costs at the same time. In the case of morale, a company can increase morale during downsizing if it starts with a clear vision to achieve that result as a possibility. In the book, *Built to Last*, by James C. Collins and Jerry I. Porras, this is described as the "genius of the '*and*,' the ability to embrace both extremes of a number of dimensions at the same time. Instead of choosing between A *or* B, they figure out a way to have both A *and* B."[5]

A vision statement tends to evolve over time. The picture that it presents becomes clearer as you move toward it, just as the details of any picture become clearer the closer you are. This is why a vision needs to be updated on a regular basis.

Create a Vision of Leadership

Vision statements are by no means limited in use to the general company; they are useful to formulate at all levels. They can be particularly useful with a leadership team that is trying to break down territorialism and become unified in leading the organization to achieve its business results.

There's nothing glib, superficial, or purely rhetorical in the following vision statement, which was developed by a leadership team at one of the leading and most innovative medical centers in the country. They

---

5. James C. Collins and Jerry I. Porras, *Built to Last: Successful Habits of Visionary Companies,* Harper & Row, 1997.

used it to become less comfort-oriented, less fragmented, and more responsive to the needs of the organization. Six months after creating this vision, their reputation with employees changed, and now the medical center's reputation in the national healthcare community is well established.

Leadership Team Vision Statement at an Award-Winning Medical Center

We, the Leadership Team, provide clear expectations to our employees, as well as the growth and development needed to meet them, and the appropriate recognition for their performance. We provide an organized structure for continuous quality improvement, effectiveness of operations, and team self-direction. The nurturing environment we create provides the information, resources, and culture of team participation needed to allow us to be continually responsive to our customers' needs.

We are a dynamic, action-oriented team willing to take risks for improvement in a responsive environment of mutual trust, respect, accountability, and support. Communication and information sharing are open, clear, honest, and uninhibited. Clearly defined processes and systems are in place to ensure the highest level of team function and to effectively deal with conflict resolution. Decisions are based on organizational needs and are accurately and consistently represented to all.

We ensure the viability of our organization by being responsive, flexible, and accountable to resolve organizational problems and barriers. We ensure that the business plan is achievable and achieved, tying operational systems to business/financial outcomes, and acting on new business opportunities. We exceed community expectations related to care, service, and culture.

How would you feel if you were part of the leadership team that developed that statement of intention and measured itself against every sentence? How would you feel if you were an employee whose leadership functioned in a manner consistent with that statement of intention?

Vision Statement for Each Department: Two Case Studies

I once interviewed a member of a work unit, Dan, who had been accused of being hostile toward his co-workers. He didn't deny his hostility; he defended it! "We never agreed to be a team," he asserted. "We never agreed to support one another. If we ever decide to do so, I'll change my behavior. But until then, I'm going to continue doing whatever it takes to get my job done."

If personal accountability means taking action consistent with one's desired

---

outcomes, then Dan was acting with personal accountability. His commitment was simply and solely to get his job done. He had made no commitment to his work group or to anyone else. Creating a vision for the department that describes the department's reputation with its customers, the teamwork necessary to accomplish their reputation, and the value of the department to the organization provides clear expectations for performance and behavior. Given a clear description of what teamwork would mean to this department, Dan could no longer isolate himself to only getting his job done. He would be expected to support the team based on the department's vision.

Another manager was complaining to me about his team. "People on my team don't support one another. They don't share information with each other, and they blame each other constantly." I asked the manager what he does about those problems, and he responded, "Nothing. If they are going to act like children, then I will treat them like children." I asked him how it was working for him. "Terrible," he replied. "They just aren't getting the message." I asked him if they ever established a vision statement that clarified expectations for supporting one another, for not blaming one another, and for sharing information. He responded with indignation saying, "Of course not. This is common sense, and I shouldn't have to spell it out for them."

After a few months, this manager was transferred. The new manager came into the same team and created a department vision statement with all of his direct reports as part of the process. When complete, his group not only raised the bar on their performance, but were now operating as the team they described in their vision statement.

Although the vision for an organization is created by an executive team and the vision for leadership is developed by the middle management team, vision statements for departments are created by the supervisors and employees of that department.

Don't Be Fooled: Goals Do Not Provide Vision

An effective vision statement is a clear picture of success that is the foundation for all business initiatives, goals, and desired changes. When the vision is vague and considered "fluff," it is viewed as ineffective for contributing to business outcomes. In those situations, organizations tend to emphasize business goals instead. However, because each division and department of the organization has different goals that they are responsible for accomplishing, the organization ends up fragmented without a clear sense of priority or direction. This fragmentation creates wasted resources, lack of coordination, and a breakdown in performance execution.

For example, a manufacturing company responded to a goal of cutting costs by downsizing employees and offering an attractive severance package to its senior and more experienced people to encourage them to leave. After the "rightsizing," they discovered that losing those resources and expertise cost them a loss of customer satisfaction and market share. A year later, they had to hire back many of the people that they had let go, because of increased demands and the need to improve sagging customer service.

> If the transition of the merged organization were based on a clear vision of excellence that incorporated a new culture with improved efficiencies and reduced costs, the typical dysfunction caused by the merger would be avoided.

Today, organizations merge for the purpose of expanding market share and cutting costs through centralization. The problem is the duplication of processes and technology that is inherited with a merge or acquisition. By creating goals to reduce expenses, effective processes are dismantled while decisions to use one process over another creates conflict and are often decided based on politics rather than on what is best for the organization. This results in wasted resources, higher costs, and poor service to customers. If the transition of the merged organization were based on a clear vision of excellence that incorporated a new culture with improved efficiencies and reduced costs, the typical dysfunction caused by the merger would be avoided.

Without a clear vision and only a focus on goals, how do you anticipate the future trends of your organization in order to prepare your skills and mind-set for the upcoming challenges you will face? How do you fit into an organization that has no sense of identity or purpose? And how do you target your responses to the organization's needs for change when the target is moving randomly from one goal to another?

The Role of Goals

Goals are necessary for translating the vision of the organization into meaningful and measurable performance objectives. However, goals must always be subordinate to the *outcomes* described in the organization's vision. Whatever your goal might be (whether it's to increase market share, improve quality, change technology, cut operating expenses, etc.), it is essential to integrate the goal's achievement with your response to other external drivers and to your values as an organization. Only then will people understand the "why" behind the goal. Only then will they be able to identify their own individual objectives for accomplishing the goal in a way that is consistent with the organization's vision.

> A vision statement sets up accountability. That is its key purpose. As long as the direction remains vague or unclear, people don't have to be accountable for changing their behavior in order to be consistent with it. Lack of clarity lets them off the hook!

Bottom Line: Accountability

Most people would agree that the purpose of a vision statement in a traditional organization is to provide a sense of direction, whereas the purpose of goals is to establish the focus for improvement or achievement. But as we've seen, if that sense of direction isn't clear, or if people become too focused on goals without understanding the context, the vision statement can become a stumbling block.

A vision statement sets up accountability. That is its key purpose. As long as the direction remains vague or unclear, people don't have to be accountable for changing their behavior in order to be consistent with it. Lack of clarity lets them off the hook! Setting a clear vision is not the cure for an organization's lack of accountability or its inability to achieve meaningful business results, but it does provide a foundation without which there would be less effectiveness and greater resistance to change. The vision provides the basis for assessing future decisions, actions, behaviors, and attitudes. It acts as an internal benchmark against which performance execution and performance improvement can be measured and modified. Without a clear vision, it is impossible to know when you are off-track so that you can correct your course.

Once the vision is clear, the challenge is developing priorities to ensure that you stay focused and clear on what you need to accomplish to be successful. In the next chapter, we will explore the process for clarifying, communicating, and monitoring priorities to ensure that everyone is working together cohesively to achieve success.

CHAPTER 7

STRATEGY #2: TRANSLATING CLEAR DIRECTION INTO NON-NEGOTIABLE PRIORITIES

MYTH: Strategic planning provides clear direction that establishes a clear focus.

TRUTH: A well-articulated set of three to ten non-negotiable priorities provides clear focus.

WHEN WAS THE LAST TIME YOU ATTENDED A MEETING and found that the focus of the meeting was the crisis of the week? In fact, if you were involved in the crisis, you were part of the discussion. If you weren't a part of the crisis, hopefully you were smart enough to bring work with you that you could accomplish during the meeting. Of course, the previous meeting was discussing a different crisis of the week, which was never followed up on. The only other activity that takes place at these meetings is the addition of new priorities, even though you are hardly keeping track of the existing ones.

To understand if an organization is clear on its direction, we ask a simple question of each executive, "What are the top five to ten priorities for your organization during the next twelve months?" Our instructions explain that we aren't looking for the top priorities for the functional area they represent, but for the whole organization. Whether the executive team is comprised of seven people or fifteen people, we generally identify between forty and sixty different priorities. The lowest number of priorities came from a small group of five executives, and they identified twenty-three different priorities.

Attempting to accomplish twenty-three to sixty priorities represents leadership's clarity and alignment on what is important to the organization. If leadership is this fragmented on their understanding of organizational priorities, how well do you think the purpose and direction of the organization is understood by others in the organization? And, we wonder why, even with strategic plans, there is such confusion about the organization's direction.

Confusion: An Organizational Virus

In an unclear environment, there can't be accountability. What would you be accountable for? Accountability requires clarity that decisions will be made, resources will be allocated or shared, and people will be developed to meet future demands. *Providing clarity is one of management's most important purposes.*

When clarity doesn't exist, you are left with confusion:

- Confusion about what is important and what is not

- Confusion about allocating time and effort

- Confusion about what information is necessary to be shared

- Confusion about where to cut costs when it is necessary to be more efficient

Worse, confusion among managers results in *miscommunication*: each manager communicates what he or she understands or desires and gives mixed messages to employees. Miscommunication to employees results in *misunderstanding*: they each come away with different interpretations of direction, what's important, and what actions to take next. This misunderstanding results in *mistrust*: Who do employees believe when they are receiving different messages? They not only can't trust the message, they can't trust the people delivering the message. This mistrust results in *alienation and isolation*, where employees feel a sense of futility, discouragement, and apathy due to the mistrust and miscommunication.

This state only adds to the confusion that remains in the organization, because everyone is now working to satisfy their own goals and needs, giving little consideration to the larger organization or its team they respective.

Identifying Top Ten Priorities: A Case Study

A mid-sized biotechnical company went through a process of strategic planning. It approached strategic planning in a comprehensive manner involving an external consultant who helped the company analyze its industry and conduct a SWOT (strengths, weaknesses, opportunities, and threats) analysis. After several months of careful analysis, senior managers identified the business outcomes and deliverables they were expecting. They identified fifty-three projects and carefully developed objectives and action plans for each. They created a committee of people just to help track each of these priorities.

Finally, after six months, the management team found that little progress had been made and that people were feeling overwhelmed and confused about the real priorities. Besides, as the business environment changed, they had added new priorities and now were up to sixty-five priorities! No wonder people felt overwhelmed.

In just a few hours of working with senior management, we had them identify the top ten priorities and established meetings to track these ten. Within six months, they had completed 80 percent of their top ten priorities and were making great progress on the other 20 percent.

Establishing the Top Ten Priorities

It is the role of executives and senior management to establish direction for an organization. As such, it is important for them to be clear on the "non-negotiable" priorities that must be accomplished for the organization to progress and succeed. Based on strategic goals, managers must agree on the top priorities to ensure alignment and focus for the rest of the organization.

We accomplish this role by having managers identify all of the possible top priorities. Next, they narrow the list down to what is most important for the larger organization. This requires each manager to step outside of the box of his or her particular line of authority and to take responsibility for the success of the entire organization. Although the organization is accomplishing more than ten priorities, the executive team (as a team) stays focused on the top ten to ensure success.

Executive and senior management teams not only create the top ten priorities, but they also identify the top two or three within the ten. This ensures a clarity of focus and allows the team to make decisions, allocate resources, and track results for the most important initiatives that ensure organizational success.

Cross-Functional Accountability

If each manager responsible for his or her own priority project accomplishes it without coordination, collaboration, and communication with others, then we are back to silos and fragmentation. Thus, it is critical at this stage to develop cross-functional accountability to achieve the organization's top priorities.

Each of the top ten priorities must have a project owner. However, the entire team of managers is accountable for the success of all ten priorities. That means if any of the projects fail, it is the entire team that is held accountable. Of course, a team or group of people can't be accountable for a result, since everyone being accountable is a kin to no one being accountable. Therefore, shared accountability needs to be described in more detail as to how it functions.

Each project owner must complete a project plan outlining in specific terms the approach he or she will use to accomplish the priority project, the challenges the owner expects to encounter, and the milestones and timelines to track progress. All of the other team members review the project plan and add their input before it is accepted. Once accepted by all team members, they must also support the implementation of the project plan.

The entire team monitors the progress of these top ten priorities to make sure the project is on track, and acts as troubleshooters and problem solvers when issues surface that might prevent the success of the projects. If one of the other managers is not supporting the project by completing an assignment or sharing information, he or she is held accountable by the other team members—including the leader of the team. Although the project owner is the point person for the priority project, it is the brainpower and support of the entire team that ensures its success.

Effective Team Meetings

The purpose of virtually any meeting should be to ensure the success of the organization's top priorities. Thus, the first task of a team meeting is to *monitor the progress of these top priorities.* This ensures continual focus on what matters to the organization. Monitoring progress takes about 10 percent of your meeting time.

Second, you must *surface any obstacles, conflicts, or major decisions that need resolution.* The team then acts as a "think tank" to resolve issues using their diverse skills, thinking styles, and perspectives. It is not the project owner who solves all problems, and it doesn't negatively reflect on him or her to surface a problem. In fact, it only reflects negatively on the project owner when the owner doesn't surface a problem and the team gets ambushed when the problem escalates into a crisis. The step of surfacing and resolving problems takes about 75 percent of your meeting time.

The third step of the meeting is to *strategize communication to others.* Once the team has made its recommendations and decisions, it must determine the best way to communicate so that the team's message is unified, representing "one voice" to the constituents (the board, community, and employees). Communication planning represents 10 percent of your meeting time.

Meetings require continual evaluation to ensure effectiveness. They are too costly to waste with ineffectiveness. It only takes 5 percent of the meeting time to assess its effectiveness and identify adjustments to be made at the next meeting. Using this meeting structure, the management team will become known for removing roadblocks, making effective decisions, and communicating effectively as a cohesive team.

Time Allocation for Effective Meetings	
10% —	Monitor Priorities
75% —	Surface and Resolve Issues (proactively)
10% —	Strategize Communication to Others (unified voice)
5% —	Assess Meeting Effectiveness and Integrate Improvements

For example, a senior management team of a 28,000-person organization completed the process of clarifying its top ten strategic initiatives. They distilled their top ten from sixty-five priorities that were part of their strategic plan. Once the top ten were clarified, one of the vice presidents made an interesting observation, "In the past six meetings, we never once discussed any of our top ten priorities because there was a crisis somewhere in the other fifty-five priorities. Clarifying our top ten priorities and establishing our new meeting process will make sure that we stay focused on what we are all saying is most important for our organization."

Six months later, we did an assessment of their progress and discovered that they had accomplished more on those top ten priorities in six months than they had previously made in the previous year. In addition, the rest of the organization was more focused on the initiatives that were most important to the organization.

The Appropriate Use of Teams for Achieving Priorities

Once the top business priorities are clear, teams must work together to achieve business outcomes. But what does it mean to function as a team? Does it mean you need to make all of your decisions by consensus? Does it mean you need to know all of the actions other team members are taking to achieve their performance goals? Does it mean you all go your separate ways and come together when all of your assignments and goals are completed?

A team's purpose is to accomplish business outcomes in the most effective and efficient means possible. The purpose of the team isn't to create an environment so people feel good working together or because it is popular. The way a team achieves its purpose is to ensure that "shared accountability" is in place so that each person completes his or her commitments of performance and communication so that all of the business priorities are accomplished.

> The way a team achieves its purpose is to ensure that "shared accountability" is in place so that each person completes his or her commitments of performance and communication so that all of the business priorities are accomplished.

This requires an understanding of how different functional areas are interdependent and must work together to achieve each of their business priorities. In addition, it may involve understanding the other priorities that each functional area is achieving to maximize coordination and collaboration. The degree to which there is interdependence between functional areas on a team determines the kind of teamwork that is necessary. In most situations, a team is made up of several teams, including teams that form and reform as priorities are being accomplished. This is referred to as "fluid" teams.

For example, a social services agency in California wanted to create more of a team structure within its organization in order to increase accountability, share resources more effectively, and improve performance. However, senior managers became stuck when a team member asked, "How do we know what kind of teams we should have? Should we be like a track team, where everyone has his or her own event but practices on the same field? Or should we be like a football team, where we coordinate each play with one another?" As a philosophy, there is no simple answer to that question. In practice, however, we can answer it by examining the organization's desired business outcomes—specifically, the priorities and projects associated with those outcomes.

First we must identify all of the functional areas and individuals who are either affected by each priority project or are needed for support in order to successfully complete the priority project. Then teams are formed based on those identified interdependencies. This ensures that those responsible for the success of the project are part of a team and accountable to each other to achieve successful results.

Figure 7-1: Priority Matrix Indicating Degrees of Cross-Functional Teamwork

Department Priorities	Finance	Training	Marketing	Sales	Distribution	Administration
1	✔		✔		✔	
2	✔	✔	✔			
3	✔	✔	✔	✔	✔	✔
4			✔	✔	✔	
5		✔		✔		✔
6	✔	✔	✔			
7			✔			✔
8	✔					
9	✔		✔	✔	✔	✔
10	✔	✔	✔		✔	✔

A formalized team doesn't mean a structured and fixed team. It means a fluid team, much like an orchestra, where members function together as needed and in an efficient and well-coordinated manner. All the instruments don't necessarily play together at the same time, but instead they contribute to the piece at different times. A soccer team provides another model. For example, only a part of the team is involved when a goal is made, even though other members of the team are there as backup and support.

To return to the question posed by the team member at the social services agency, the decision about what type of team to form is less important than the exercise of determining the necessary interdependencies among the team members for achieving their priorities. Figure 7-1 indicates the interdependence across functional departments for a set of business priorities needing to be accomplished. As you can see, some priorities will require a higher degree of teamwork and interdependence than others. An organization with a higher level of interdependence will also require a higher level of accountability as outlined in the accountability continuum in chapter 1 (refer to figure 1-1 on page 5).

The Misuse of Teams for Accomplishing Priorities

Like many improvement programs that enjoy popular appeal, teams are often misused by organizations. In some cases, this misuse is destructive; in others, it is merely counterproductive. Teams have been used by managers as a way to avoid coaching or disciplining the non-performers. They use the "team process" to mobilize co-workers to deal with a nonperformer on the team. The result is that no one deals with the nonperformer, and now the entire team resents the manager for avoiding his responsibility.

Teams are sometimes called "committees" or "task forces" to complete special assignments. Although some committees and task forces provide a positive and productive purpose for getting results in an organization, others are set up as an avoidance tactic. We all know of at least one organization which, anxious to make a change without taking on the responsibility for communicating the "bad news," decided to "empower" employees to form a committee that would study the problem, make a recommendation, and implement a change. Then the employees could be blamed for the change rather than management. Naturally, this type of manipulation undermines trust.

Another misuse of teams is as a vehicle to eliminate an entire management level by "empowering" a team of employees to manage themselves. Initially, the team will probably welcome its new autonomy. But rarely is the team provided with a clear direction or with coaching. Later, the team finds it has no representation in the organization for getting more resources, it is left out of meetings that impact their performance, and individuals are not provided development opportunities for advancement.

> When organizations use teams to build morale, improve relationships, empower employees, or transfer accountability from managers to employees, the results are usually short term at best.

When organizations use teams to build morale, improve relationships, empower employees, or transfer accountability from managers to employees, the results are usually short term at best. Teams can produce these kinds of positive results on a short-term basis; however, sustainable impact comes when teams are focused on clear business outcomes with clear priorities.

For example, a large governmental agency wanted to build greater trust and communication within its management team. In an effort to create a team environment, the management team participated in ropes courses, style assessments, team-building sessions, and other activities. After two years, their relationships with one another had improved, but their team functioning hadn't changed. They still weren't accomplishing their goals as a team, and they were still fighting each other for resources. Focusing on how they related to one another missed the real objective of how well they worked together to achieve clear business objectives. Teams are only a means to an end, not an end in and of themselves.

Conclusion: How to Make Teams Effective

The purpose of teams within an organization is to achieve the highest levels of performance execution. Performance execution requires the coordination, communication, and decisions that impact several people at once. Teams need to be unified in their direction and also in how they will work together to accomplish their goals and deliverables.

What are the keys to effective performance execution? What kinds of development do teams need to have before they can be high performing? What are the keys for developing "fluid teams" that achieve benchmark results? The next chapter will answer these questions and discuss one of the most critical elements for achieving high performance and accountability.

CHAPTER 8

STRATEGY #3:
EXECUTION: THE KEY TO
HIGH PERFORMANCE

MYTH: The purpose of team development is to improve relationships and morale.

TRUTH: The purpose of team development is to improve *accountability* and *performance execution to achieve business outcomes.*

A S AN ELEVEN-YEAR-OLD KID IN SIXTH GRADE AT A PUBLIC SCHOOL, I had one of my first team experiences outside of sports or music. Influenced by my grandfather, a practical joker, I devised an April Fool's joke to play on my teacher. It wasn't hard to convince two of my friends to go along with the gag. The plan was to hide ten significant items from our classroom, including the teacher's desk, a set of encyclopedias, and other impressively large objects, so that when she walked in the empty room she would be shocked.

First, we planned the event. We identified which objects would disappear and the process for returning them. Because we had been studying poetry, we decided to present our teacher with rhyming clues to help her find each object. We also decided how we would decorate the room. We intended to have a party after she had successfully located all the missing items, and we decided what food and drinks to have. In addition, we identified the key people whose support we required, including the school principal. Not only did we need his permission, but we also needed him to let us in the room before school to hide everything and set up the decorations. Because of all the work involved, we decided to expand our committee by another five students.

We had so much fun. Everyone had a role and did their job on time even though it was a lot of work. We shared information effectively to maintain the necessary secrecy and to complete our tasks. We had a great plan and coordinated our activities smoothly. We didn't need to understand each other's style, though we used each other's strengths and interests to complete the various tasks. Although the prank had been my idea, we all participated in the leadership of this event. Everyone was aligned, and there was no territorialism or fighting about who would take on certain tasks. We all cooperated as a team with a high level of trust, even though we had never participated in any ropes courses or team-building exercises. Our communication was effective even though we hadn't attended a course on communication. Even our classmates who weren't involved were supportive and kept their accountability by keeping it a secret.

As eleven-year-old kids, we successfully designed, planned, and implemented a fabulous April Fool's event long before we understood the meaning of the words "design," "plan," and "implement." We had a clear purpose and participated fully. We counted on each other for support, guidance, effective communication, and keeping our commitments. Our accountability formed the backbone for our teamwork, and our teamwork provided the backbone for our success.

Performance Execution: The Missing Piece to Achieve Breakthrough Results

Before the introduction of the Quality Movement, high performance was achieved by building the skills of each individual in the organization. If a breakdown occurred, a person or group of people were "blamed" and then sent to a training program to gain skills in their area of deficiency. The assumption was that if everyone in the organization was highly skilled, we would have a high-performing organization.

Once the Quality Movement took hold, we changed our paradigm from blaming *people* to blaming *processes*. We assumed that if operational processes were streamlined and employees were skilled, we would have a top-performing organization. Process and skill are not enough to attain top performance.

In 2004, I watched Olympic basketball. The team from USA was the strongest in terms of individual skills and reputation. Yet, Argentina won the gold medal, and Italy won the silver medal. All three teams had streamlined processes (plays) that they all practiced prior to and throughout the competition. So, what was the difference between these three teams if wasn't skill and streamlined processes? Performance execution. Improving skills and streamlining processes are only a small part of how teams win and why teams practice. They practice to improve their performance execution as a team, which ultimately is the most important factor in winning ballgames.

They practice to improve their *execution* of performance—to refine how they function as a team. Even the best ballplayers on the best teams must improve their linkage with each other—their performance execution. This involves improving their communication, fine-tuning their coordination, and adjusting their timing in order to develop the highest performance possible. Ultimately, their execution is what determines how effectively they score and avoid being scored against.

The same is true for a professional orchestra. All the musicians must be highly skilled—that goes without saying. They wouldn't have secured a job in a professional orchestra if they were not highly skilled. What they're rehearsing is how *seamlessly* they can perform together. Music critics often comment on precisely this ability when reviewing symphony concerts or recordings.

We streamline our *technical* processes, but not our *team* processes. We fail to review the linkage and accountability among individuals and departments. This lack of focus on performance execution results in the breakdown of projects, the duplication of resources, and the existence of conflicting priorities between departments and/or people. Accountability breaks down, not because of a lack of skills or technical processes, but because of a lack of "shared accountability" and tracking systems to ensure that linkages take place among various performers. Figure 8-1 illustrates what these linkages should look like.

Figure 8-1: High Performance

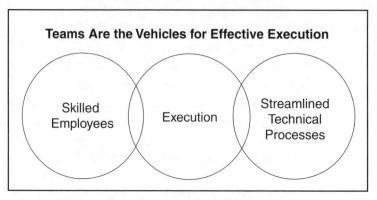

Teams Are the Vehicles for Effective Execution

Skilled Employees

Execution

Streamlined Technical Processes

Teams Are the Vehicles for Effective Execution

Recently, I received a phone call from a Boston-based client who wanted to tell me about the latest improvement program being piloted in her organization. "We're piloting the use of teams in our organization to determine if it will work in our culture," she said. This organization was a highly technical research-oriented institution that relied on the sharing of information, the coordination of projects, and the utilization of limited resources. To ask the question of whether or not teams would work in this culture was to miss the point.

In most organizations, teamwork is not an option. It already exists. As long as two or more people are sharing information, making decisions, or coordinating activities, team structure is already in place. Whether it is *effective* or not is another story. These are the issues of performance execution that need to be "practiced" to become effective. Peter Senge emphasizes the importance and value of teams in his book, *The Fifth Discipline*: "Team learning is vital because teams, not individuals, are the fundamental learning unit in modern organizations. This is where the 'rubber meets the road'."[1]

Without having teams focus on how they execute, the team ends up dysfunctional and slow to respond—just as any athletic team or music group would be if they decided not to practice. When teams do review and upgrade their execution and recovery, high performance and breakthrough results become the outcome. As Senge reminds us: "When teams

1. Peter M. Senge, *The Fifth Discipline*, Currency Doubleday, 1990.

are truly learning, not only are they producing extraordinary results, but the individual members are growing more rapidly than could have occurred otherwise."

Teams of people working together represent the place in an organization where performance execution must be exhibited to create an accountable culture and to achieve breakthrough results. James M. Kouzes and Barry Z. Posner make a great case for this in their book, *The Leadership Challenge*, where they report the following: "In the more than 550 original cases that we studied, we didn't encounter a single example of extraordinary achievement that occurred without the active involvement and support of many people. . . . People continue to tell us, 'You can't do it alone. It's a team effort.'"[2]

> Teams provide the mechanism for creating true accountability—an environment in which people can count on each other for their performance and positive relationships.

Unfortunately, most teams leave out the accountability factor. If they do any team development, it tends to focus on different personality styles, general communication skills, awareness activities to emphasize the importance of teamwork, and visioning processes to create alignment. Although these bits of knowledge and experiences are helpful as background, when the *real work* of a team needs to be accomplished—i.e., the work that involves sharing critical information, coordinating priorities, making decisions, and managing conflicts—the team finds itself without the shared accountability or the habits of performance execution necessary to function. For example, a basketball team cannot execute a "fast-break" effectively by learning about each other's styles, gaining the skill of active listening, or experiencing the values of teamwork by solving a team-building puzzle. The team must *practice its execution* of the "fast-break" repeatedly to achieve high performance.

Teams provide the mechanism for creating true accountability—an environment in which people can count on each other for their

2. James M. Kouzes and Barry Z. Posner, *The Leadership Challenge: How to Keep Getting Extraordinary Things Done in Organizations*, Jossey-Bass, 1995.

performance and positive relationships. This goes beyond the hierarchical form of accountability, where employees are accountable only to their bosses. In a true team, members are also accountable *to one another.* But most organizations aren't structured to support the teamwork necessary for effective performance, nor do they have the processes in place to ensure that the teamwork that does exist results in bottom-line results.

Performance Execution Represents the Habits of an Organization

Improving performance execution has been an ongoing challenge for most organizations. We treat performance execution as a skill, offering training programs in decision making, managing conflict, and communication. While training is useful and effective for helping people to develop their individual skills, it generally falls short when attempting to change the organization's culture. Generally, training doesn't address performance execution in its entirety.

For instance, in a manufacturing company, people would avoid conflict and talk negatively about others behind their backs. This not only caused low morale, but it also caused breakdowns resulting in inconsistent quality and poor customer service. The company wanted to correct this problem, so its senior managers required everyone in the organization to attend a workshop on conflict management and having difficult conversations. Managers and employees learned the skills of communication, active listening, win-win dialogues, and open body language. While a few employees tried their new skills, most reverted back to "old habits" cemented in the culture of the organization when they returned to the organization, thus avoiding conflict in the same way as before. People didn't feel safe to use their new skills with others. In fact, some people even used their new communication skills to make an even stronger case against someone behind their backs!

Performance execution represents the *habits* that an organization has developed for years. It is often referred to as, "the way we have always done things around here." Many organizations have bad habits, such as:

- Avoiding with nonperformers

- Excluding affected parties when making decisions

- Withholding information openly

Organizations can have good habits as well, which typically include:

- Tracking measurable results

- Conducting fair hiring practices

- Soliciting feedback from employees about their levels of satisfaction

It is critical to explore the habits of performance execution that currently exist in an organization and determine which of those habits are having a negative impact in achieving business outcomes, so that they can be changed. In general, we don't change a habit simply by learning a new skill or gaining a new awareness. Here are some guidelines for how to change your organization's habits:

1. You have to replace our old habit with a new one.

2. In a team or organization, changing habits depends on creating alignment and commitment toward adopting the new habit.

3. Because organizational habits involve the *linkage between people*, changing habits must be accomplished in groups or teams.

4. As with the change of any habit, the new habit must be repeated continually and measured for the purpose of staying focused.

5. And, when people go back to old habits, they must have a recovery plan for getting back on track.

6. Finally, it is critical to measure the impact of changed habits on performance outcomes.

How to Change Your Habits of Performance Execution

Although ropes courses, experiential retreats, and training programs can raise the awareness of working in teams and understanding the impact people have on each other, by themselves, they rarely change habits of performance execution. Changing habits of performance execution to raise the level of team performance is achieved over time in a systematic way that is tracked and measured until the new habit becomes "the way things are done in this organization." The following three steps are used to improve performance execution.

Step 1

Develop a Team Vision of Excellence—A Stretch

Before we explore habits of performance execution, your team must be clear and in alignment about your meaning of excellence. Using the approach discussed in chapter 6, your team develops a vision statement representing the highest levels of excellence regarding your reputation with customers, your teamwork, and your value to the organization. This picture of success gives you a clear idea of where you want to be as a team and what it looks like when you get there. It is clear and descriptive and provides the mind-set for establishing the habits of performance execution.

For example, an operations department was fragmented. People were working at cross-purposes, and unresolved conflicts turned into a culture of blame and lack of trust. In addition, customer satisfaction was low. People in this department were more interested in protecting old dysfunctional ways of operating rather than changing for the better. They had the reputation in the organization for being the lowest performers.

Working with this department, the first activity was to create a vision of excellence that described the kind of reputation they wanted to have.

Vision for an Operations Department

The operations team works as an integrated unit. Each team member plays his or her own position; however, team members cover for other team members in order to serve our customers. Team members promote trust by actively supporting one another, communicating openly, and keeping commitments. As a high-functioning team, each person handles a multitude of projects at once and has the ability to prioritize the projects according to the critical needs and time frames of our customers.

As priorities shift, the team mobilizes its strengths in response to changing needs, optimizing activities to complete the tasks in the most efficient manner possible. Our efficiency and high level of quality is what drives our team. We are in constant communication with the involved or affected customers to coordinate and update the progress of the project.

The atmosphere in the office is enthusiastic, energetic, professional, relaxed, and confident. Customers view us as highly professional and a model of teamwork. Each member challenges the others to their highest level of performance. It is a fun team to be a part of due to its continual success, and is respected as a model support staff team.

Once this vision was created and agreed on by all members of the operations department, they had a clear sense of the kind of team they wanted to be. This represented a "new mind-set" for how they would be functioning in the future. However, they didn't have the *habits* of performance execution to support the new vision of excellence that they all aspired to.

Step 2

Develop Success Factors of Performance Execution

Once the vision was clear, the team identified a list of Success Factors of performance execution, which describe in detail everything that the team would be doing to fulfill their vision. These Success Factors of performance execution represented their "ideal habits." The operations department created them by answering the following question: "If you were already accomplishing your vision at the highest level of excellence imaginable, what would it look, sound, and feel like on your team?"

Success Factors are expressed in terms of statements that describe specific behaviors that reflect the highest levels of performance, coordination, and communication. They may include such qualities as:

- Efficiency
- Customer service
- Project management
- Cross-functional relationships
- Safety
- Quality
- Documentation
- Communication

- Tracking and measuring results

- Follow-through

- Decision making

Success Factors are not goals; they are success *criteria* from which goals can be developed. In a sense, Success Factors represent the "blueprint" for success of an organization or team. They are a set of criteria by which the organization or team must function to achieve its desired outcomes. They are the desired habits to achieve successful results.

Success Factors are key for turning a vision into reality. It takes most teams less than two hours to come up with between twenty and thirty different Success Factors representing all aspects of performance execution. As a blueprint for success, it is time well spent.

Samples of Success Factors from the Operations Department

1. Scheduling changes that arise are quickly and effectively communicated to others who may be affected by the change.

2. Our work areas are orderly and free of clutter so that even those unfamiliar with our work area can easily find what they need.

3. All projects are logged onto the job board upon receipt, and we immediately review the scheduling for conflicts and reprioritize jobs as necessary for maximum work flow and minimum crisis.

4. We stay well educated on leading-edge technologies and techniques for streamlining our operational processes by attending classes and seminars, by acquiring and studying texts, and by subscribing to and reading a broad range of technical magazines and periodicals.

5. We proactively pursue input and feedback from customers, and we regard any unsolicited opinions they may offer as constructive criticism and an opportunity for improvement. We respond to customer feedback with openness, action, and a message of gratitude to our customer for offering input or feedback.

6. We embrace challenges with a "How can we meet the challenge?" approach, rather than focusing on all the aspects of the challenge that are difficult.

7. Even when our processes are working efficiently, we are continually looking for methods of improvement.

8. Each of us regards personal growth and improvement as the core of our organizational, team, and individual success; and in that spirit, we openly turn to others to both request and offer coaching and support.

Success Factors include both the "soft" side of performance execution as well as the more quantitative or "hard" side of performance execution. These two sides of performance execution are demonstrated in the sample of above. Success Factor #3 describing project scheduling represents a "hard" side of performance execution. Success Factor #6 describing an attitude of problem solving represents a "softer" side of performance execution. Success Factor #2 describing an orderly work area is a combination of a "soft" and "hard" side of performance execution. Representing the softer and harder sides of performance execution is effectively described by James C. Collins and Jerry I. Porras as the "genius of the *and*."[3]

Like many other teams that have developed Success Factors, the operations department used them as criteria for hiring new team members, assessing individual employee performance, and providing a source of team recognition. Of course, as the operations department improved its performance, the employees in that department saw opportunities to increase the standards described in their Success Factors as they continued to raise the bar on their performance.

Step 3

Prioritize Success Factor Improvement Goals

Once Success Factors of performance execution were agreed on by all team members, each team member chose the top three Success Factors he or she felt would have the biggest impact if improvement took place. As a result, the department agreed on three Success Factors that they turned into *improvement goals*. Although two of the Success Factors involved performance issues, the third success factor was focused on communication. Team members developed action plans for improving each of the chosen Success Factors and agreed to review progress at each of their team meetings.

When we came back six months later to measure results, they had improved eight of their ten Success Factors (70 percent), and four of ten (40 percent) were significant improvements. This included the three Success Factors that they chose as improvement goals. The measurement

3. James C. Collins and Jerry I. Porras, *Built to Last: Successful Habits of Visionary Companies*, HarperCollins, 1994,1997.

was done as a "blind" subjective rating, meaning that they didn't look at their previous ratings when they re-rated the Success Factors. Two years later, they were viewed by their organization as one of the top-performing and model departments.

Improving Performance Execution Leads to Measurable Business Outcomes

Which team do you think will win more games: the basketball team that practices its coordination and timing for executing defensive and offensive plays, or the team in which each person only practices shooting baskets? The team that practices performance execution will, more often than not. The organization that focuses on performance execution (making decisions more effectively, coordinating projects and activities within those projects, and sharing information openly and appropriately to achieve project goals) will outperform the organization that only focuses on measurable indicators for success and pushes people to work harder to achieve those goals. This has been demonstrated for several years, and now there is data to support what makes common sense:

In the year 2004, all of the management teams that committed themselves to the process of changing their habits of performance execution achieved an average of eleven out of twenty-five Success Factors each improving by 24 percent or higher within six months. When Success Factors of performance execution improve to this degree, business results are also impacted.

Three companies in three different industries demonstrate the impact of improving performance execution on achieving business results.

PHARMACEUTICAL BUSINESS UNIT

Success Factors of Performance Execution

- **Surfacing and Solving Problems:** As a team and in discussions, we challenge the status quo to engage conflicting opinions in order to generate constructive conversations to drive a uniform resolution and resolve critical business issues. (improved by 24 percent)

- **Act on New Business Opportunities:** With clear direction and focus we are proactive in defining/researching/identifying/ understanding the business climate and opportunities. We seek out information using every avenue. We select best possible people/resources to execute. We overcome lack of resources— no victims. (improved by 71 percent)

- **Clear Direction and Focus:** We take control of the situation. We set immediate goals (twelve months) that align with long-term vision (five years) (agreement, buy-in, total commitment). We define (clearly) the direction and how our goals support that direction. We communicate clearly defined goals. We focus on the goals aggressively to completion where failure is not an option. (improved by 57 percent)

Business Results

- Improved spending to budget by $2.5 million (9 percent under budget)

- Increased sales by 22 percent from the previous year

- Reduced FDA observations from seventeen to three

MEDICAL CENTER

Success Factors of Performance Execution

- **Customer Service:** We continually evaluate the needs of our customers by survey, feedback, and meeting with them so that we might better anticipate and exceed their needs and determine their expectations. (improved by 47 percent)

- **Fiscal Responsibility:** We will use the revenues we receive to provide services to our community by managing our budgets and working together as a team to reduce costs, share resources, and increase efficiencies. (improved by 57 percent)

- **Sharing Information:** Giving and receiving of pertinent information is done openly and honestly between all team members in a timely manner. The means of communication (e-mail, phone, memo, meeting, etc.) is utilized as appropriate in order to prevent wasted time and effort. (improved by 33 percent)

Business Results

- Reduced operating costs by more than $4 million in three months through cross-functional problem solving at middle management

- Achieved their highest scores by a regulatory agency in the history of the organization

- Improved patient satisfaction by 25 percent

ENERGY PLANT

Success Factors of Performance Execution

- **Cost Awareness and Control:** We view all expenditures as if it came from our personal checking accounts. We actively challenge the presumptions of benefit to the organization and the customer of each dollar we spend and spend only those where benefit is assured. (improved by 13 percent)

- **Demonstrating Success:** We continually strive to achieve successful results related to milestone completion, effective cost/budget estimating, budget status awareness, and equipment reliability while maintaining a focus on regulatory compliance and safety. (improved by 24 percent)

- **Cross-Functional Relationships:** We assess our customer/ teammates' needs and constraints and seek solutions so that we all succeed/win. We establish cross-disciplinary teams when appropriate. We share information with our teammates (outside our silo) as much as we do inside. We praise and celebrate other's successes (publicly) and challenge/criticize privately. We measure success by what *WE* accomplish rather than what *we* accomplish. We communicate accurately. (improved by 24 percent)

- Reduced lost time rate related to safety issues by 22 percent

- Reduced average safety corrective action scores from 900 down to 116, breaking all previous safety records

- Corrective maintenance backlog is down by 25 percent

Changing Habits of Performance Execution Leads to Sustainability

Although the measurable results demonstrated above are impressive given the relatively short time frame of six to nine months, what is more impressive is the *sustainability* of those results. For example, consider these successes:

- A medical center that has been using this process for more than ten years has sustained benchmark status in its industry, regularly hosting site visits so that other medical centers can learn about how their accountable culture continues to produce high-performance results, productivity, and profitability.

- An IT department dedicated to accountability increased customer satisfaction (including the achievement of awards), and morale improved by 25 percent in the first nine months and maintained those ratings over a five-year period. Since that time, it has had continual improvements in customer satisfaction, and morale has continued to increase in a linear progression.

When accountable organizations develop new habits of performance execution, they typically report continued improvement in job satisfaction and business outcomes for more than five years.

What are the habits of performance execution that are most linked to your business outcomes? What habits of performance execution are working for you and which ones would you like to change to achieve breakthrough results? What are the costs associated with the dysfunctional habits of performance execution that relate to silos and territorialism, to wasted resources, and to loss of your high performers?

The organizations listed here that achieved breakthrough results did not demonstrate perfect performance execution. They made mistakes. They had breakdowns. They experienced crisis. The difference was that they developed the skill of *proactive recovery* to make sure they could get back on track in a way that was transparent to their customers. The next chapter focuses on developing this skill of proactive recovery.

Chapter 9

STRATEGY #4: PROACTIVE RECOVERY: THE SECRET TO ACCOUNTABLE PERFORMANCE EXECUTION

> **MYTH:** Focusing on perfection results in sustained high performance.
>
> **TRUTH:** Focusing on proactive recovery, while striving for higher levels of excellence, results in sustained high performance.

Proactive Recovery: The Secret Behind High-performing Execution

WHAT DO TOP-PERFORMING BASKETBALL TEAMS FOCUS ON when they practice? *Proactive recovery.* The coach sets up "what-if" scenarios in which the team must deal with the unexpected. What happens when things break down? What happens when the team's outside shots aren't going in, or when its star player gets hurt? The coach makes sure that the team practices its ability to *recover* when various breakdowns occur. Everyone develops the skills to respond to difficult situations, as well as the ability to mobilize the team to recover from breakdowns in the most effective manner.

Dr. Benjamin Carson employs a similar principle in his operating room. A legend in the medical community, he was named chief of pediatric neurosurgery at Johns Hopkins Hospital in Baltimore in 1984 at the age of thirty-three, becoming the youngest American doctor ever to hold such a position.

Three years later, he made history by leading the first successful operation to separate Siamese twins joined at the head. Today, he performs up to five hundred operations annually, which is double the caseload of most neurosurgeons. One of the ways he handles the pressure is by playing classical music in the operating room. Another way is by planning for problems. "[I] focus clearly on what can go wrong," he says. "I think through every procedure; how I expect it to go, how long each phase will last, when I can move on to the next one. But the real value of planning comes when things don't go the way I expect. I always anticipate the worst-case scenario: What's the worst thing that could happen? What can I do to make sure it doesn't? What will I do if it does?"

Contingency plans in organizations are rarely given the attention they deserve. Project planning meetings will address the project outcome, the benefits, the strategy, and the action plan and still somehow miss identifying the potential breakdowns. Too often when a breakdown occurs, people are caught off guard. They panic, sometimes fleeing from the situation, creating yet another problem that begins to snowball. Some projects are measured on their ability to achieve perfection without a problem. Some project managers I have encountered don't believe in recovery plans because that would be an admission that there were problems and would create a negative affirmation that allows for breakdown.

The team with the fastest and most effective recovery will be the highest performing team. Its members can respond to both crisis situations and to changes most effectively, because they are best equipped with the *flexibility* required to continually adjust to change and unforeseen situations that take place.

Generally, when you become overly concerned with perfection, you will make more mistakes. Have you ever tried to watch every movement you make while you are climbing a set of stairs? You will probably trip.

In figure 9-1, you can see what happens in the dynamics of an organization. Performance seems to be fine. Then, a breakdown occurs and performance drops. When the organization emphasizes *perfection* to the point that people feel punished for making a mistake, then *hiding* takes place. You don't want someone to find out that you made a mistake so you try to correct it before anyone notices or try to hide it so that no one finds out. Then, performance continues to go down until it becomes a crisis. Now, everyone knows about the mistake, and several people have to get involved to correct it. The good news is that by getting everyone involved, the breakdown is solved and performance goes back up. The problem is the length of time that you operate in the gap between high-performance standards. Figure 9-1 illustrates the continued drop in performance when people hide their mistakes in fear of management's reaction. It also illustrates that organizations are crisis-

Figure 9-1: The Performance Gap When Problems/Mistakes Are Hidden

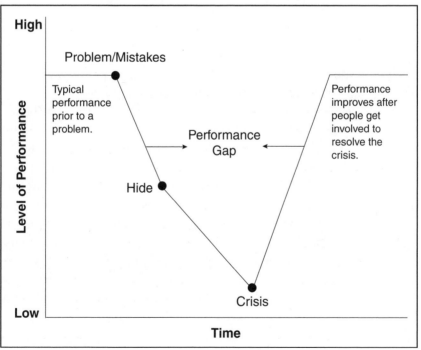

Figure 9-2:
Sustained Performance Through Proactive Recovery

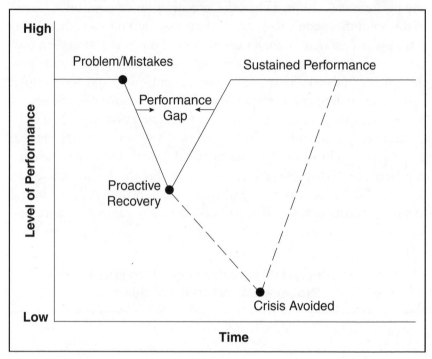

oriented if they continue to operate at a level where people wait to get involved only when a problem becomes a crisis.

In an organization that focuses on proactive recovery, the same breakdown can occur. It will cause the same decrease in performance results. However, without fearing mistakes and with the establishment of a recovery plan, we implement our recovery process, involving the appropriate people, earlier. The breakdown gets resolved right away, and performance is back to normal. Although most organizations only focus on perfecting performance, the high-performing organization also focuses on reducing its recovery time to make it as seamless and transparent as possible. This results in *sustainable* high performance. Figure 9-2 illustrates the impact of proactive recovery on preventing crisis and sustaining high performance where the impact of problems or mistakes are minimal.

There is a story about one of the *Phantom of the Opera* productions that demonstrates proactive recovery in motion. During a live East Coast performance, the boat that was used at the end of the performance broke down. Rather than stopping the performance and giving the audience their money back or tickets to another performance (which would also have demonstrated high-customer service), the show went on. The actors immediately went into recovery mode—they changed their lines and their blocking on stage just as they had rehearsed in case of such an occurrence. They removed the broken boat and replaced it with their recovery boat. This all happened without the audience knowing it. To the audience, it was a perfect performance. To the actors and stage-hands, it was a less-than-perfect performance with fantastic recovery.

In the book *Corporate Lifecycles: How and Why Corporations Grow and Die and What to Do About It*, Ichak Adizes describes the difference between "young" and "old" organizations: "'Young' means the organization can change relatively easily, although what it will do because it has a low level of control is fairly unpredictable. 'Old' means there is controllable behavior, but the organization is inflexible; it has little propensity to change."[1]

Developing recovery systems enables the organization to be both flexible and controllable, making it neither too young nor too old. These are skills that are only learned with practice. By focusing on recovery during team development sessions, teams can work out the "plays" ahead of time. Each member of the team will know how to coordinate efforts, use resources, and communicate effectively, trusting that other team members will carry out their predetermined roles and functions

This goes far beyond the standard fare of typical team building. Proactive recovery focuses on *shared accountability*, where the team practices how they will function together in order to accomplish their desired results.

The Five Stages of Recovery

When a problem surfaces, either a team can recover by surfacing the problem and responding as a seamless operation, or drag out the problem by hiding and blaming others for mistakes. To create enough "safety"

---

1. Ichak Adizes, *Corporate Lifecycles: How and Why Corporations Grow and Die and What to Do About It*, Prentice Hall, 1988.

Figure 9-3: The Five Stages of Recovery		
Stage	Title	Description
1	Self-correction	We look for, find, and resolve our mistakes.
2	Observation by Co-worker	Co-worker points out a problem with our performance, and we self-correct.
3	Coaching by Co-worker	Co-worker points out a problem and assists us in improving our performance.
4	Coaching by Manager	Manager points out a problem and assists us in improving our performance.
5	Corrective Action by Manager	After coaching has failed, manager implements a corrective action process to either improve performance or to find a new team player who will perform.

for people to admit mistakes, raise concerns, and hold others accountable, it is useful to understand the five primary stages of proactive recovery, shown in figure 9-3.

Stage 1: Self-Correction

We've already explored how the organization with the fastest recovery will be the highest performing organization. So, specifically, what can you do to improve your recovery time? First, you have to *become aware* that a problem exists. The sooner you realize that a problem exists, the faster you can recover from it. The fastest way to do that is for you to be aware of your own mistakes as soon as they occur. This takes commitment to a level of personal excellence that keeps you looking for opportunities for improvement. Although self-correction is desired, it is humanly impossible for us to always recover at Stage 1. (In our book *The Power of Personal Accountability*, we outline in detail the steps for self-correction using the "personal accountability model.")

Unfortunately, you can't always see when you're making a mistake, or when you're not performing optimally. Maybe the clarinet player in the orchestra plays a B-natural instead of a B-flat in bar 135, realizes it, and corrects himself the next time the passage is performed. But suppose it is an atonal piece, hence his "ear" is no longer recognizing the misplayed note as incorrect. What then?

Stage 2: Observation by Co-Worker

The next fastest route to recovery is to have a team member observe and point out the problem to the person who is responsible for it. The conversation in the clarinet section might go something like this:

"How come you're playing a B-natural in bar 135?"

"That's what's written."

"No. It's a B-flat. Look!"

"That's amazing! You're right. The first time that passage comes up it's a B-natural, but here it's a B-flat. How could I have missed that?"

And you can be sure he won't miss it the next time.

Too often, though, what happens in organizations with vertical accountability is that team members are reluctant to point out errors to one another for fear of hurting egos or seeming disloyal. There is no "safety" in doing so. Instead, team members cover for one another, and perhaps they grumble about it privately. It is more comfortable to *provide support* for our teammates who make a mistake than it is to *criticize* them.

Stage 3: Coaching by Co-Worker

Sometimes when your performance is less than optimal, you don't know how to recover on your own. In an accountability-based organization, a team member will offer to provide guidance or coaching. Maybe the clarinet player isn't just playing a wrong note. Maybe that piece contains a highly complex rhythmical pattern that he just doesn't "get," and consequently, he keeps missing his cue, which throws off the second clarinet player sitting next to him. In this scenario, the second clarinet player might offer to work with him on that passage or give him a tip that will help him.

Again, many organizations are not set up for this type of coaching, which instead is often viewed as "interfering." Without a safe environment for this type of feedback and coaching among team members to occur, the team's performance will rarely be optimal, no matter how much people like, trust, and respect one another.

Stage 4: Coaching by Manager

Sometimes team members don't cooperate with one another either in their linkage or in their own individual performance. At other times, they just aren't in a position to learn from one another. Their styles may be different. In this case, it is necessary for the manager to step in and provide direct coaching. The manager offers his or her perspective, skill, encouragement, and the articulation of clear expectations and deadlines. This is where recovery begins in many organizations. By the time the manager finds out about a problem and responds, it may be too late to prevent major breakdowns resulting in missed deadlines or wasted resources.

Stage 5: Corrective Action by Manager

If the problem continues, the leader needs to move into corrective action with the specific nonperforming team member to ensure that his or her performance improves and that he or she becomes a contributing team member. This corrective action process involves documentation as well as contact with human resources to ensure fairness both to the employee as well as to the employee's co-workers. At this point, you not only aren't achieving high performance, you risk survival.

A "Stage-5" Case Study: Corrective Action by Manager

An architecture design company's small executive team consisted of a CEO and his five vice presidents. During interviews that occurred before our intervention, the CEO complained that his vice presidents didn't take enough initiative and that their follow-up was weak. The vice presidents, in turn, complained that the CEO didn't give up authority.

During our intervention, we introduced a nonwork related activity (assembling a puzzle) to see how they would function together. Each person was given one piece of the puzzle, and the team had to fit the pieces together to form the puzzle within three minutes, and without talking to one another. When the exercise began, each member of the team passed the first test by giving up their piece of the puzzle to the rest of the team, to allow everyone to move all the pieces. Each member, including the CEO, passed the second test by managing to come up with different options to form the puzzle but without dominating the team. However, they still weren't successful in putting the puzzle together. I then announced that there was only one minute left so that I could see how they would react under pressure.

Suddenly, upon that announcement, the CEO stood up and pulled all the pieces of the puzzle in front of him. For the next forty-five seconds, the CEO worked by himself to put the puzzle together, while the vice presidents watched.

Low Performance and the Breakdown of Recovery

Most organizations aren't set up to initiate recovery before reaching Stage 4, the stage at which the manager must become involved. Can you imagine an athletic team or music group that had to wait for the coach or director to find and surface every performance problem on the team? They would no longer be top performers, that's for sure.

Even when the problem involves the entire team, people are still reluctant to bring up the issue for resolution. So everyone pretends it doesn't exist until the manager raises the issue or until it becomes the topic of discussion for a "task force" focused on the next quality improvement program. So long as organizations support a system of vertical accountability, they will not provide sufficient safety for co-workers to support each other by raising issues for the purpose of resolving them.

Many managers are reluctant to provide coaching and guidance. Some have abdicated their role under the guise of "empowerment," expecting employees to improve on their own; whereas others avoid the discomfort by giving poor performers a satisfactory score on their performance review as long as they promise to do better next time. Several years later, when the poor performers haven't improved, they are transferred to another department where the process repeats itself. This is another example of a dysfunctional habit of performance execution that prevents achieving the highest standards of excellence.

When a leader fails to deal with a performance problem, everyone loses. The poor performer never improves, which ultimately catches up with him or her, possibly in the next downsizing. Additionally, his high-performing teammates must increase their own efforts in order to maintain an effective operation. But even they cannot cover for a weak teammate indefinitely. Anyone can have a bad day, and other team members must be prepared and equipped to accommodate those bad days.

But when one team member is chronically having bad days, no room is left for other team members to have their bad days. Ultimately, the high-performing team members will break down in their efforts to make up for the chronically poor performance of their teammate.

Likewise, the team's approach becomes less than optimal because it has to compensate for a weak link. This is like jogging with a limp: after a while, the good leg collapses under the added strain. The team experiences stress, burnout, and eventually dysfunctional performance, ultimately leading to self-doubt. Ironically, it is at this point that leaders often implement a team-building effort to try to solve the problem, though their avoidance of their own leadership role as coach to the nonperformer continues.

> On any high-performing athletic team or music group, team members are accountable to each other whether they are at different pay levels or at different levels of seniority.

Instead of running away from performance problems, you need to address them as quickly as possible. The faster you address a problem—whether it involves a technical process, team process, an individual's performance, or some other problem—the less painful it is for everyone.

Shared Accountability: The Key Ingredient for Quick Recovery

In the past, we blamed the traditional hierarchy for preventing organizations from performing effectively. We tried to develop more effective organizational structures, such as matrix organizations, flat organizations, or business-unit organizations. However, after restructuring, people would still function in their territorial and controlling posture. The problem is not with the hierarchical structure. The problem is with the way we operate *within* the structure—how we've defined the "ground rules" for functioning level to level, department to department, and individual to individual.

We define the functioning of the hierarchy in terms of vertical accountability, where a person is accountable to a manager, who in turn is accountable to another manager. Unfortunately, vertical accountability by itself can never be optimal because it limits accountability to the next manager or leader in the hierarchy. Rarely does it allow for accountability to the people affecting us the most—our co-workers.

On any high-performing athletic team or music group, team members are accountable to each other whether they are at different pay levels or at different levels of seniority. Each team member is accountable for setting and keeping agreements, for supporting one another, for holding each other accountable when agreements aren't kept, and for challenging one another to strive toward their next level of successful performance. This doesn't *replace* the leader's role; rather, it functions *in addition to* vertical accountability. It is effective in a hierarchical organization or a matrix organization or a business unit.

We call this "shared accountability," which means that we are accountable to everyone we have an impact on regardless of their position, level, or function. Shared accountability demands that you are accountable for your performance and relationships and for holding others accountable when agreements are broken or a breakdown occurs, as shown in figure 9-4.

Figure 9-4:
Shared Accountability Model

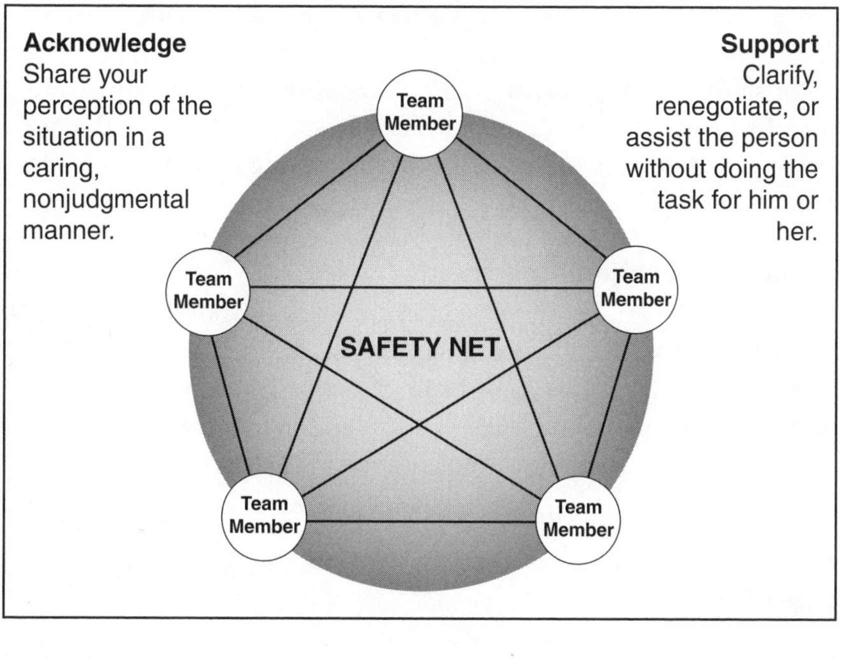

Acknowledge
Share your perception of the situation in a caring, nonjudgmental manner.

Support
Clarify, renegotiate, or assist the person without doing the task for him or her.

Team Member

Team Member

Team Member

SAFETY NET

Team Member

Team Member

In organizations, people generally do one of the following:

1. Ignore the person responsible for the breakdown and talk behind his back to every other team member hoping that he'll get the message without knowing who has sent it

2. Blame the person for being a bad team member

Both cases promote victimization and separation rather than team-work.

In contrast, shared accountability functions through acknowledgment and support. If a breakdown occurs, you acknowledge it without judgment, and you offer assistance to the person responsible, without actually solving the breakdown for him. In *Leaders: The Strategies for Taking Charge*, Warren Bennis and Burt Nanus refer to acknowledging people without judgment as one of the key skills of leadership: "The ability to accept people as they are, not as you would like them to be. In a way, this can be seen as the height of wisdom—to 'enter the skin' of someone else, to understand what other people are like on their terms, rather than judging them."[2]

When you greet mistakes with *acknowledgment and support* rather than *blame and punishment*, you create the safety and accountability to con-tinually work on improving performance, and to deal with crises head on.

In short, the new paradigm maximizes performance by increasing the speed and effectiveness with which a team recovers when things go wrong. They don't have to wait for the manager to become involved for the recovery process to begin.

Develop Interaction Agreements

To ensure that performance isn't interrupted by relationship issues such as unresolved conflict, miscommunication, and a lack of trust, high-performing teams create their own Interaction Agreements. These so-lidify the practical operational relationships among people, functions, and departments. They determine how conflicts will be resolved. They

---

2. Warren Bennis and Burt Nanus, *Leaders: The Strategies for Taking Charge*, Harper & Row, 1985.

represent how team members will work together in all aspects of their functioning and relationships. These include agreements regarding:

- How information will be shared

- How team members will be supported by one another

- How decisions will be made

- How trust will be maintained

Interaction Agreements are *not* just guidelines for behavior. Most of us tend to abandon guidelines when the behaviors are less than perfect. Interaction Agreements include a set of conditions for acceptance that incorporates all the behaviors associated with keeping an agreement. The conditions also include recovery systems for the times when an agreement is broken and behaviors less than perfect.

Although it may take an hour for a team to hammer out several solid Interaction Agreements, it will save hundreds of hours of time spent later in stifled processes or unproductive meetings stemming from unresolved conflicts, a rehashing of issues, incomplete tasks for important projects, or lack of participation.

Interaction Agreements provide the process for reinforcing shared accountability. To remain effective, Interaction Agreements must be reviewed at team meetings on a regular basis to ensure consistency and accountability. If people are failing to keep their agreements, they are held accountable with *acknowledgment and support* consistent with their recovery process and in a manner that encourages *team alignment and unity*.

For instance, a team had an agreement that "If any team member had an issue with another team member, he would speak with the person directly to resolve the issue." David, a team member, continued to break this agreement. At the next meeting when the Interaction Agreements were being reviewed, Gloria spoke up, "David, I have noticed that you have come to me several times when you have had an issue with another team member. I have been directing you to talk with the appropriate team member who is directly involved. Is there anything else we or I can do to support you in going to the person directly without going to any other team members first?" In this case, Gloria demonstrated acknowledgment when she described the situation without judgment against David. She then demonstrated support when she asked David if he had ideas for directing the team to support him in making a change to be consistent with the agreement. In this case, David asked to have one member on the team act as a "sounding board" for him, so that he would present himself well to the team member in which he had an issue. The team added a condition for acceptance to the agreement allowing for a "sounding board."

Acknowledgment and support is not only used when agreements are broken, but also when agreements are kept. At a team meeting one month later, Gloria recognized David for his improvement on the agreement.

As demonstrated in the example above, sometimes an agreement must be changed for practical reasons or because the team isn't ready to demonstrate the level of trust required by the agreement. Because this process is an evolutionary one, Interaction Agreements must be revised over time. It is not uncommon to witness a team increasing their levels of trust 15–45 percent within a six- to twelve-month period through the use of Interaction Agreements.

Ultimately, the goal is to create teams in which members have the safety to challenge each other in a supportive way and to surface and resolve conflict without getting stuck in hurt feelings, resentment, or retaliation. Once teams know how to recover with grace, speed, and a unified focus, no crisis or change is too great to handle. Figure 9-5 shows a sample Interaction Agreement.

Figure 9-5: Interaction Agreement Example

Guideline:

Each team member will freely express his or her opinions and feelings along with the explanation for those opinions/feelings during team discussions.

Conditions for Acceptance:

a. People will ask questions to better understand your position, rather than ask questions to make you appear wrong or put you on the defensive.
b. No retribution from anyone on the team.
c. No holding a grudge.
d. Don't share humor at the expense of respecting each individual or their ideas.
e. If you feel put down, or aren't sure of people's intentions, raise the issue.
f. Focus on issues, not the person; disagree with respect.
g. Demonstrate understanding for another person's point of view before disagreeing.
h. Don't act on assumptions; ask questions or check out your assumption.
i. No attacking of others or their programs.
j. Don't over-talk the needs/problems within your department or go on tangents.
k. Don't speak for someone else's position.
l. Don't line up votes or lobby outside of the meeting related to Leadership Team issues.
m. If you feel someone is over-talking or on a tangent or that lobbying has taken place, bring it up to the team for direction.
n. If someone is approaching you to lobby a vote, remind him or her of the agreement.

Win-Win Interaction Agreements: A Case Study

An information systems and technology department for one of the top-rated public universities in the United States was structured into five separate areas. Each area performed autonomously, and within each area, individuals were also autonomous. At the same time, their customers regularly complained that they were out of touch. They didn't share information when problems occurred, and they had major malfunctions during times of transition.

This department developed a clear intention for effective performance along with a set of Success Factors that identified the functional behaviors necessary for success. It also established a set of Interaction Agreements for ensuring that co-workers were able to resolve conflicts, make decisions, and coordinate the sharing of information and resources.

After six months and an improvement of 83 percent on their Success Factors, the team also received glowing reports from their customers. There were no quality breakdowns, there was more problem solving taking place with customers directly, there was an increase in cross-functional problem solving, and there was a large reduction in costs. Not only was the team performing at higher levels of quality and efficiency with a smaller staff (due to outside influences), but also morale in the department increased by 25 percent, according to a standard climate survey that had been used for several years.

The team members were unanimous in their response to the question of what contributed most significantly to their success: "We now have a recovery plan both for our projects and for our relationships. If anything goes wrong, it doesn't cause a crisis; it just mobilizes us to respond in a planned way to get results despite problems. We work better together, assisting and coaching one another, and we achieve greater results at the same time. Everyone wins!"

CHAPTER 10

STRATEGY #5: CREATE A PLAN FOR CHANGE THAT GUARANTEES RESULTS

MYTH: The more we *perfect the plan*, the more employees accept and are comfortable with change.

TRUTH: The more we *plan for recovery*, the more employees accept and are safe to take the risks of change.

HAVE YOU EVER WONDERED why so many change efforts fail? You create perfect plans involving several groups of people. You develop beautiful presentations to communicate the change, and you even provide elaborate training programs to build people's awareness and skill in the change. Yet, with all of your great effort, you find that the change takes longer than expected, people still resist, and many times the change doesn't achieve the business results or culture change that you were expecting.

What is the missing element? *Accountability*.

There's a popular misconception that if we *involve people* in the planning of change, they will *feel accountable* for that change. There is nothing further from the truth. Just because people are involved in planning a change effort doesn't mean that they will feel accountable for the change.

For example, a large petrochemical company was planning to re-structure from being organized in centralized functional departments (maintenance, human resources, and information technology) into cross-functional business units, where each plant contained its own dedicated maintenance, human resources, and information technology staff. One division involved large numbers of employees in several groups to study the change and make recommendations. Their goal was to include people so that they would "buy into" the change, take ownership, and be accountable for achieving results.

Another division in the same company making the same change involved only a few people in its planning. The leadership team instead focused on providing clear direction with clear understanding for the change. They didn't sell the change and told people up-front that it was going to be challenging. They guided people through the change and involved them in the implementation.

The first division involving large numbers of people took one year to move from planning to implemen-

> It is essential to have an environment where people "can count on each other" so that information is shared effectively, decisions are made in a timely manner involving affected parties, and coordination of execution takes place smoothly.

tation, and by that time, there was so much resistance that the change was postponed for another six months.

The second division planned the change in five months and completed implementation inside of one year, reporting improved performance and improved morale. They exceeded expectations and increased accountability within the organization—even though less people were involved in the initial planning.

What are the keys to planning and implementing change in an accountable way to get results faster with less disruption to morale?

Six Stages of an Accountability-Based Implementation of Change

Whether the change you are planning involves organizational restructuring, introducing new technology, or implementing a culture change, there are certain steps that must be followed to ensure accountability during the change process. It is essential to have an environment where people "can count on each other" so that information is shared effectively, decisions are made in a timely manner involving affected parties, and coordination of execution takes place smoothly. Including people in the change without following the steps to ensure accountability creates breakdowns that prevent success. In this case, you are setting people up for failure.

As the stages for accountable implementation of change are discussed, you must understand the *impact* of each stage of change on the person experiencing the change. Why? Because there are "typical" reactions that are normal for people to experience. If you overreact to what people experience during a change effort, you may cause them more harm rather than being helpful. Also, having a better understanding of what people experience enables you to be a better coach to effectively lead people through change. Figure 10-1 illustrates typical reactions many people experience at each stage of implementation of an accountability program.

One of the common traps you can get into is moving on to the next change effort before successfully completing the existing one. It is too easy to move on to the next change effort before successfully completing the existing one. This results in sabotaging your results and leaving the people involved in the change discouraged. It is like taking the time to prepare and cook a gourmet dinner but not staying around long enough to enjoy the meal.

Some stages are self-explanatory. In this chapter, we will focus on the keys most often missed for effective implementation at each stage, and we address specific reactions to these changes that require special attention.

Stage 1: Planning the Implementation and Communication Strategy

Planning is an essential step in any project or change effort. However, with so many failed projects and the degree of resistance from employees,

---

the tendency in recent years has been to "perfect" the plan prior to implementation. Certainly, when an organization is planning the purchase of major capital equipment or construction of a building, it is appropriate to take the time to perfect the plan as much as possible, because recovery is difficult once the commitment is made. However, most projects and change efforts aren't so predictable, and the lengthened planning process can be detrimental to effective implementation.

Don't Plan Your Way to Failure

What's worse than getting bad news? *No* **news.** When we don't know where we stand in relation to our situation or our relationships, we feel out of control and enter a state of fear. Anyone who has ever waited for the results of college entrance exams, job applications, or medical tests knows how difficult the not-knowing period can be. When

Figure 10-1: Reactions to the Stages of Implementation		
STAGES OF IMPLEMENTATION	**TYPICAL REACTIONS ➤**	**WHICH CAN TURN INTO**
1. Planning the Implementation and Communication Strategy	Fear ➤	Negativity
2. Leading Through the Initial Accountability-Based Implementation	Chaos ➤	Confusion
3. Clarifying Roles and Relationships	Cooperation ➤	Frustration
4. Tracking Milestones and Making Modifications	Clarity ➤	Discouragement
5. Communicating Results	Optimism ➤	Disbelief
6. Recognizing Success and the People Involved	Confidence ➤	Accomplishment

you know that changes are going to be made in your organization, but you don't know the impact on you personally, you may experience anxiety or fear. When it is a restructuring, you could fear losing your job. Even if your job is secure, you may wonder if you will be asked to perform a new function that you don't feel confident about. Furthermore, in a "no news" situation, you tend to imagine the worst.

The longer we are in a "no news" situation, the greater our fear. Our imagination starts working overtime, fueled by stories about the negative experiences of others. A project or change that is still being planned is, by definition, a "no news" situation. We know that a change is imminent, but we don't know how it will impact us directly. By extending the planning period in order to create a more perfect plan (which we hope will make people more comfortable), we are actually *increasing* people's fear about the change. In fact, when the planning stage extends too long, fear can turn into rebellion. This was the case in the petrochemical company described earlier in this chapter.

The other downside to "perfect" planning is the impression it gives that if anything goes wrong with the plan, the people implementing the plan must be at fault. This creates even more fear and resistance from employees.

Finally, if our focus is on perfecting the plan, we often fail to even think of developing the recovery systems necessary for effective implementation. This means we have become attached to the plan based on how we *think* it will go, rather than leaving ourselves *flexible* to adjust as necessary to achieve our desired outcomes. This "detachment" is referred to by Deepak Chopra as the "sixth spiritual law of success" in his book, *The Seven Spiritual Laws of Success:* "The Law of Detachment says that in order to acquire anything in the physical universe, you have to relinquish your attachment to it. This doesn't mean you give up your intention, and don't give up your desire. You give up your attachment to the result (as you planned it)."[1]

Becoming "detached" to our plan enables us to stay open when the unexpected takes place and adjustments are necessary.

1. Deepak Chopra, *The Seven Spiritual Laws of Success: A Practical Guide to the Fulfillment of Your Dreams*, Amber-Allen Publishing and New World Library, 1993.

Figure 10-2: Traditional vs. Accountability-Based Planning

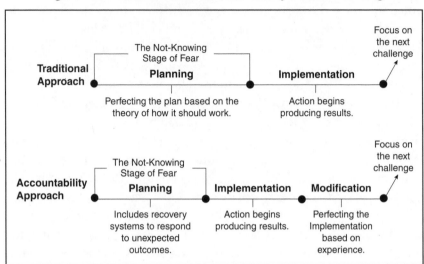

Accountability-Based® Planning: A Shortcut to Success

Figure 10-2 illustrates the benefits of accountability-based planning. Notice that the time involved is the same for both traditional and accountability-based planning. But accountability-based planning requires a shorter planning stage and involves the development of recovery systems. By focusing more on the development of recovery systems than on the perfection of the plan, we have been able to reduce the time required for planning by up to 50 percent. Consequently, fear is reduced and implementation takes place sooner. This means that results become evident sooner as well. The "extra" time can then be devoted to modifying the implementation based on experience rather than theory.

It is impossible to perfect any plan without first taking action. Although we can't anticipate all the problems that might surface, we can establish contingency plans and ways to mobilize resources when problems do surface. Focusing on recovery eliminates the worry that people will be punished for mistakes. This frees them up to concentrate instead on developing responsive and timely solutions.

Nowhere was this better demonstrated than in the space expedition to Mars in the spring of 1997. The computers were down and needed repair while the expedition was in progress. Fortunately, recovery had been a critical part of the planning process. Heroes emerged among those individuals who were ready to respond to such a challenging and unpredictable situation.

Nine Steps to Creating a Plan that Achieves Results

Step 1

Define a Clear Outcome

Prior to initiating a plan, it is important to have a clear picture of success. What will be accomplished once the implementation is complete?

Step 2

Determine Measurable Indicators for Success

It is important to have as many different measurable indicators for success as possible. These could involve indicators for the business as well as indicators for morale. The measurable indicators are necessary for acknowledging success afterwards and assisting the "naysayers" to come into alignment with the change.

Step 3

Identify Success Factors of Performance Execution

It is important to have a clear idea of what needs to happen during the change effort in order to ensure success afterwards. This means developing clear statements describing what it will look like to be accomplishing and implementing the plan successfully.

For example, one Success Factor could include making sure that affected parties are included in the brainstorming of solutions because they will eventually be impacted by the change. Another Success Factor could be developing a clear communication plan and orientation program for getting people to understand their role in the change effort.

Step 4

Set Milestones and Timing for Success

Once we understand the outcomes and the Success Factors, it is important to create a set of completion targets that will indicate whether or not the implementation is on track. Milestones present a road map for accomplishing the plan and provide the means for tracking the results as progress is made. For example, I wouldn't make a cross-country trip by car from Los Angeles to New York without first knowing which cities I would be stopping at along the way, and the timing of those stops.

Recognize Challenges, Obstacles, and Constraints

Identifying the challenges that could arise in the future is one of the most important aspects of a successful plan. Too often, we wait until implementation begins to identify obstacles, only to find that it is too late to deal with them.

Once these challenges are identified, we can determine the ones that are within our influence and those which aren't. If there are too many obstacles, we may decide to trim down our expectations and the scope of our plan in order to prevent failure.

Step 6

Take Actions to Achieve the Milestones

Once the milestones and obstacles are clear, we can identify the actions that will accomplish the plan. These actions must not only assist in achieving the first milestone, but they must also be proactive to address future milestones if appropriate. Also, these actions must address the obstacles discussed earlier.

Step 7

Develop a Recovery Process

This is one of the most important steps but one that most often gets forgotten. What kinds of problems may occur that we can't predict? What if several unpredictable obstacles happen at the same time? A recovery plan identifies various types of breakdowns, including performance breakdowns, relationship breakdowns, and changes occurring from outside of the project. Then, a recovery plan is established that identifies what resources are needed and how they will be mobilized to get back on track to successfully complete the plan.

Step 8

Assign Follow-up Accountability

Once a plan has been documented, it is important to establish a regular follow-up system to ensure that each milestone is being completed on time as agreed. It would be too detailed to review every action item, but reviewing the milestones gives you a sense of progress or breakdown. If a milestone is not completed on time, the team can review the supporting action items that are not being accomplished to find alternatives or resolve breakdowns. Of course, this is where the team may turn to one of their recovery plans for a quick resolution.

Step 9

Evaluate Results and Recognize Who's Responsible

Once the implementation is complete, it is critical to measure the results in comparison with the desired outcomes. With this information, we can acknowledge success and the people involved, and we can examine areas that could have been smoother so that performance can be improved next time. Ultimately, it is this step of the plan that will turn nonbelievers into believers.

Once the nine-step planning process is complete, the next critical and often overlooked piece is the development of a communication strategy to inform others of the plan for achieving results. I have seen some project initiatives take three to six months to communicate, and at the opposite extreme, other initiatives are communicated immediately by e-mail. Both methods are ineffective:

- Taking too long to communicate the plan creates more confusion than clarity, especially because many project solutions or changes aren't understood until actual actions are taken that allow people to experience the results. Also, taking an overly long amount of time to communicate the plan only further extends the planning period, which increases the state of fear.

- On the other hand, communicating an important change via e-mail or some other form that does not allow for back-and-forth dialogue leaves people's questions unanswered, creating confusion, frustration, and resistance.

Communication is not an *event*. It is an *ongoing process* that needs to be delivered throughout all stages of implementation. It should be coordinated in such a way as to produce a unified message. A good communication strategy is based not on how well you *share* information, but on how well you *manage the inevitable reaction* to that information. (We will discuss the communication strategy in greater detail in chapter 11.)

> Communication is not an *event*. It is an *ongoing process* that needs to be delivered throughout all stages of implementation. It should be coordinated in such a way as to produce a unified message.

Finally, whenever you make plans that you fail to implement, you create an environment of negativity that undermines confidence in your ability to lead. The CEO of a major manufacturing organization announced the initiation of a new continuous improvement program in order to increase performance and stimulate employee involvement. However, when the CEO decided to abort that program less than three months after the announcement, there was a major drop in performance and morale, not to mention his credibility.

Stage 2: Leading Through the Initial Accountability-Based® Implementation

Implementation requires much teamwork, support, and cooperation. Yet managers frequently "empower" others to implement their "perfect" plan, only to find themselves with stalled efforts and failed results.

Hiding Behind Empowerment

"We have studied the problem at great length, developed an in-depth plan, and now *you* are empowered to implement the plan we have given you."

Does that sound familiar? Not only do you feel a little lost by the change that catapults you out of your comfortable way of performing the job, but you also feel abandoned by management, which has now empowered *you* to solve all the problems when, in fact, you still need direction and guidance from *them*.

After planning comes action, and the sooner action is taken, the better. Bear in mind that no matter how well you plan, the initial stage of implementation will be chaotic. Chaos is inevitable because, at this stage, people are either implementing new processes, working with new people, or using new technology. Whenever you do something new, you must expect a learning curve until you are proficient. You'll be slower than you were before the change was implemented. You'll be awkward and will make mistakes as you adjust to the changes. Yet, during this stage of awkward, slow learning, you will still have customers to satisfy and they will still be expecting the same level of responsiveness and quality as before. You will feel pressured as well, which adds to the turmoil.

Such chaos is consistent with the laws of nature. Imagine you are sitting in front of a still pool of water. Drop a pebble into the water and observe the chaos. Then watch the chaos settle down into ripples radiating out from the place where the pebble entered the water. Now toss a second pebble into the water so that it disrupts the pattern of ripples. Chaos ensues once again. But before long, even the two sets of ripples settle down into a new and predictable pattern.

> Bear in mind that no matter how well you plan, the initial stage of implementation will be chaotic.

Lead Through Chaos and Crisis

Recovery plans help us to shift from being reactive to being proactive when an organizational change is introduced. An unexpected problem occurring in the initial stages of implementation can easily turn the chaos into complete crisis. However, if recovery systems are created during the planning stages, people will be prepared for crisis and cope with it much more effectively. The good news about chaos and crisis is that at least they shift our focus from paralyzing fear regarding the full range of "what if" scenarios into action regarding the "what is" scenario. A focus on recovery helps turn the confusion and surprise of chaos into predictable actions, and this has a calming effect on everyone involved.

Many projects or change efforts come to a halt after initial implementation where change is announced and movement begins. Managers either begin planning the next project or react to the crisis caused by the existing one. This causes problems about three months into the implementation when the crises are diminishing and people have settled into new routines. People now find themselves confused about the real differences created by the new processes of the change effort.

Though processes, technology, or teammates may have changed, people find themselves conducting their same job in a way similar to how they performed prior to the change. This is when the goals of the project or change effort are most at risk and likely to be compromised; people have a tendency to return to their old ways of doing things. Some examples are as follows:

- Managers who have been reorganized into a team are still making decisions autonomously.

- A newly formed cross-functional team of employees is still withholding critical information to achieve better results on the job.

- Employees forget what it was, exactly, that the project or change effort was supposed to accomplish. They're not sure about their new roles and relationships, and they realize they can do their job in a way that is similar to the old, comfortable way. Without making a conscious decision to do so, they slip back into their old habits of behavior and attitude.

The net result, when the project or change effort stops after implementation, is that three to six months later, people will see their effort as having been superficial or a waste of time.

Stage 3: Clarifying Roles and Relationships

Although general roles and relationships are addressed at the beginning of Stage 2, they need to later be clarified and refined to reach an even greater level of detail now that people have had a chance to experience the realities of the new situation.

Success Depends on Effective Linkage

A manager complained about the difficulties of project implementation in her organization. I mentioned that one of the keys to successful implementation is to clarify roles and relationships. She assured me that this stage had already been completed. But I knew from her descriptions of the confusion and the breakdowns of teamwork that we were not talking about the same thing when it came to clarifying roles and relationships.

Her description of this step went on as follows: "Everyone on the team was brought into a conference room. They took turns reading aloud their job roles, job descriptions, and job duties. Everyone asked questions about everyone else's responsibilities to gain a full understanding of the project." Although this might have been a good starting point, it didn't address or clarify the *linking relationship* between each role.

It is critical to determine and clarify how people are going to function differently with each other in their new roles. This involves dissecting the linkage between people. Although I may know what your responsibilities are in your new role, I don't know what information you need from me, or what decisions must involve you. At this stage, expectations are clarified, boundaries are discussed, and needs are articulated and discussed.

This is the time for team members to create agreements for performance execution: namely, how they will share information, resolve conflicts, make decisions, and hold each other accountable when they fall back into pre-change patterns of behavior. They then establish a means of monitoring their results as a team by establishing specific milestones that demonstrate progress made. When this stage is missed, you can find yourself and your team stuck in old dysfunctional habits of performance execution and with unresolved conflicts.

> It is critical to determine and clarify how people are going to function differently with each other in their new roles. This involves dissecting the linkage between people.

Stage 3 is when accountability for making the change takes place. Confusion is now replaced with a sense of *cooperation* and *collaboration*.

Clarifying expectations, and understanding how we will function together, result in a sense of teamwork not often experienced in organizations. Now that the linkages we depend on to achieve high performance are in place, we no longer feel that our lack of performance is the result of another team member's lack of cooperation.

But we're not finished with the change process yet. Stopping at this stage will eventually result in frustration. Until you put the process outlined here into practice, you can't know for sure if the agreements you've made are the ones you need to function effectively as a high-performance team. Most likely, you will need to modify, or at least fine-tune, your agreements and your relationships based on the practicalities of the workplace. For example, one team member may become unable to attend meetings because of her travel schedule, whereas another may not be available to participate in all decisions because she will be out in the field. If these adjustments aren't made, then everyone grows frustrated in the wake of another failed agreement, and they experience the misunderstandings, hurt feelings, and resentments that arise when the team is breaking down.

Stage 4: Tracking Milestones and Making Modifications

Although accountability is established in Stage 3, it becomes operational in Stage 4. Accountability is tested when mistakes are made or when systems or agreements break down. Do people quit? Do they attack one another? Do they ignore problems? Or do they immediately surface issues and problems along with solutions? Do they hold each other accountable in a supportive way to get back on track? Without milestones to measure progress, many projects or change efforts lack the accountability necessary for full success.

Have the Guts to Face Breakdowns

Based on the agreements developed in Stage 3, regular meetings are held to monitor milestones and modify processes, functions, and relationships. Now is the time to see what is and is not working based on tangible expectations and measurable results. We need regular opportunities to surface breakdowns, so we can discuss them and solve any problems that have arisen.

During these meetings, decisions are made with clear actions and commitments to taking those actions in order to improve performance. Agreements regarding the functioning of the team are reviewed and modified. Any lack of accountability is surfaced and discussed in order to achieve greater success and an even higher level of support during the next period.

An odd phenomenon takes place during Stage 4, which is generally about five to seven months after the change has been implemented. Every team and organization we have worked with has experienced a state of discouragement during Stage 4. In its manifestation, it can be as obvious as depression or as subtle as apathy. Strangely, it doesn't seem to make any difference how successful the project has been in terms of well-defined measurable results; people still tend to experience discouragement at this stage. So far, there has been no way to prevent this reaction. The only antidote seems to be to move on to Stage 5, where it is addressed.

Stage 5: Communicating Results

One reason that we become discouraged during our change efforts is because we focus so keenly on what needs modification and improvement. Month after month, we examine what isn't working and consider how to make modifications to improve results. It's understandable how we can become discouraged. Implementation always gives rise to problems that were not anticipated or included in the plan.

Beware of the Discouragement Trap

I worked with a team that was frustrated because their conflicts were never acknowledged, and thus could never be resolved. The members were tired of the hidden agenda that was part of every communication. No one felt safe. So we created a process for surfacing and dealing with conflict in a more supportive manner.

When I returned three months later, they complained that things were even worse than before. Luckily, I'd had them complete a survey before we started and then once again at this follow-up session. I showed them the results of the surveys, which indicated that they had, in fact, significantly improved their levels of trust, communication, participation, and conflict resolution. They realized that they had forgotten what it was like before. As one member shared, "Now that we are surfacing and dealing with our conflicts, it just appears that we have more conflict than ever." The other members agreed.

After a few minutes of discussion, the group grew noticeably optimistic about their progress as a team. Encouraged by their measurable improvement, they wanted to take on many more performance objectives now that they had demonstrated the ability to work through their differences.

With change efforts that involve more tangible performance criteria, the illusion of failure is even more prevalent. Figure 10-3 indicates how, as time progresses, the positive energy that comes from solving the most immediate change-related problems turns into discouragement and apathy. The honeymoon is over. A similar phenomenon occurs after people marry, after we purchase a new home, or after we get a new job. And for some reason, it usually takes place around six to twelve months after a major change.

This corresponds to another trend that we have identified. The measurable and tangible results of a change effort are actually at their highest levels about six to twelve months after the project or change is implemented. This is because it takes a certain amount of time for results

Figure 10-3:
Attitudinal Shifts 6–12 Months After a Major Change

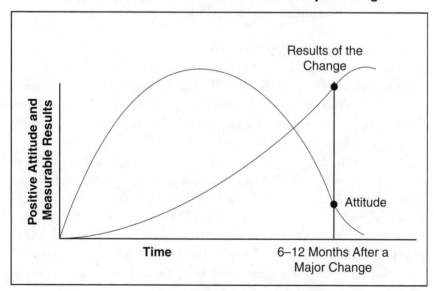

to become evident. During initial implementation, when people are experiencing chaos and crisis, the results are minimal. Results increase dramatically as they build on one another. However, because our focus in Stages 3 and 4 is on those areas requiring the most improvement and having the highest rate of failure, we can become discouraged.

The Importance of Keeping Score: A Case Study

A few years ago, I helped to implement a change within a large petroleum company. It was having problems related to performance and productivity. We set up milestones, expectations, and agreements for making improvements. In addition, we identified more than one hundred unresolved conflicts between different departments around performance execution, processes, and procedures. I was scheduled to return in March to measure their progress.

In February, they reported that they hadn't had enough time to implement the changes they had committed to, so we rescheduled our follow-up for May. In May, they called to reschedule the follow-up for August, giving me the same excuse. It was clear to me that they were discouraged and didn't want to face their perceived failure. I was reminded of a comment by one of my coaches: **"You may think you are losing when you are actually winning, if you don't keep score."** I knew that I had to take a strong stand and visit in May as scheduled or risk the discouragement that sets in six months after a change effort.

When I arrived, they completely changed my schedule, to prevent me from doing my follow-up assessment. After readjusting my schedule and finally conducting my assessment, we discovered that 60 percent of the performance expectations that had been identified showed *significant improvement.* In addition, 55 percent of all unresolved conflicts were *completely resolved* as agreed by all parties both separately and privately. This shocked upper management as well as the rest of the organization. But the most amazing results were in the tangible changes that had taken place since the implementation of change. Each manager could demonstrate *measurable improvements in organizational performance and productivity.*

Given their level of discouragement, how long do you think it would have taken for them to abort this change and start another change effort, which would lead to even greater frustration and discouragement? Now we can see another reason why "flavor-of-the-month" changes take place in organizations. Often people don't realize just how much improvement has actually occurred.

Communicating the results is the most critical step for sustaining measurable and meaningful improvements and keeping employees motivated and encouraged during implementation. If we stop short of this step, people will begin to discount the measurable results and to question their validity. This is when disbelief sets in within the minds of those involved in the project or change effort.

Stage 6: Recognizing Success and the People Involved

After communicating the organizational results of the project or change, it is important to draw the link between those results and the measurable business outcomes that formed the basis of the project. This step adds meaning to the effort and reminds people of how the intention of the organization relates to external drivers, internal values, and the mission of the organization. Nothing is more motivating than being part of an organization that can demonstrate that it has accomplished its clearly stated purpose through a well-coordinated and unified effort. Everyone shares a great sense of accomplishment when the organization succeeds through determined actions as opposed to just pure luck of the marketplace.

The Essential Element of High Morale: Making a Difference

It is important to recognize the *results* prior to recognizing the *people* who achieved those results. Otherwise, the recognition is empty. For example, some groups have been recognized for their effort only to discover that they didn't get results and now don't have a job.

Ultimately, people want to know that they have made a difference. Simply being told you did a good job doesn't tell you that your efforts made a difference. Once you understand the impact your efforts had on creating meaningful changes, you really appreciate recognition for those efforts and for the contribution you made to the organization's success. As part of this recognition, it is critical to acknowledge the breakdowns that occurred and the recovery processes that people used, because this best illustrates their level of commitment and dedication to excellence. This is also a time to reinforce the linkages that were created between people, levels, departments, and functions in order to ensure success.

In short, it is essential to link these changes made in the culture to the measurable results that indicated achievement of business outcomes. This comprehensive approach to recognition builds trust, commitment, and motivation, and it delivers a clear message to those employees who are not yet aligned with the transformation.

Recognition not only brings a sense of closure, it also inspires in people a sense of accomplishment that will carry them into the next project or change effort. By posing the organization's vision statement as the basis for recognition, we provide people with an update as to the next set of habits that need to be transformed. This second set of changes, however, will flow naturally from the previous project rather than stand alone as yet another separate and fragmented "flavor-of-the-month" project. Most important, based on their earlier successes in overcoming obstacles, people at all levels emerge with a feeling of confidence, an understanding that perfection wasn't necessary, and a sense of self-empowerment to tackle the next change effort with less fear and resistance.

Chapter 11

STRATEGY #6: COMMUNICATE TO INFLUENCE "NONBELIEVERS"

MYTH: Change should not be implemented without buy-in.

TRUTH: True buy-in comes *after* implementation, when people have experienced the results of the change.

WHEN MY DAUGHTER WAS SIX YEARS OLD, SHE BECAME ENAMORED with the idea of ice skating. She had never skated before but was inspired by the ice skaters she saw on television during the Olympics. She begged us unrelentingly to take her skating and after a couple of weeks, we did. When we arrived, she was excited but a little overwhelmed by the different environment of the cold rink. Her first setback was putting on her skates, but that was nothing compared to the struggle she experienced when she tried to stand up. That's when she informed us that she didn't want to skate anymore. She demanded that we go home.

Knowing that she had a history of not liking new activities at first but loving them after getting used to them, we told her that we were planning to stay until she tried to skate. At the same time, I reassured her that I would be on the ice with her to hold her up and make sure she wouldn't fall. She was resistant and shed some tears, but this was typical for her when trying something new. We went around the rink once, and she cried most of the time, but she didn't fall. I complimented her on her courage and persistence and told her I was proud of her. Based on our agreement, we accommodated her request and went home.

The following weekend I decided to take her ice skating again, because I didn't want her to leave this sport with a bad feeling or with a fear that would prevent her from trying it again. This time she cried again but was receptive to a skating lesson. Although she continued to cry during the lesson, she managed to skate across the rink all on her own without falling down. Again, I complimented her on her progress and success, and her courage to keep trying even though she was crying.

By the end of the month, her crying had been replaced by laughing, joy, and well-deserved pride: she now counted up to ninety-four times that she had skated around the rink on her own without stopping or holding on. Although skating has not become her favorite activity, she overcame her fear to the point where she enjoys it enough to ask us to take her four or five times a year.

My daughter's desire was to skate. But even with that desire, she still had to move through her own wall of fear. Once the fear took over, she didn't want to skate anymore. Like most of us, once fear takes over, she stopped moving toward her desired goal. The only way for her to overcome her fear was to get on the ice and skate. No amount of watching other skaters on television or reading stories about skating was going to reassure her. By taking action one step at a time, with safety and guidance, she was able to be successful. This was her *accountability in action*.

The Moment of Truth: When the Plan Turns into Action

Almost anyone who has worked in management in the past decade has, at some point, been part of an implementation planning team for a major change initiative that has impacted every person in the organization. We've all "been there," and it probably looked something like this:

- You spent several months analyzing the situation, researching different approaches for improving the situation, and solving the issues that created the need for the change in the first place.

- You involved people from all levels of the organization and even included external experts to make sure you hadn't missed anything that could potentially cause failure.

- You understood all the factors that went into the philosophy behind the change.

> No matter how much time is spent planning, if the implementation plan is poorly communicated or is misunderstood, it will result in complete failure, and you will have to abort the effort and start all over.

- You solved problems and dealt with conflicts regarding different approaches for implementation.

- You were confident that the plan was well thought out, with supporting data and clear steps for implementation.

- Then you faced the moment of truth, when the plan turned into action.

This is where the rubber meets the road. You know that your proposed recommendations will impact the lives of many people, including yourselves. You have no idea how people will react or respond to your recommendation. What you do know is that communication of the implementation plan may be the single most important factor in determining its success or failure. No matter how much time is spent planning, if the implementation plan is poorly communicated or is misunderstood, it will result in complete failure, and you will have to abort the effort and start all over. No wonder you lose sleep worrying about how to communicate in a way that generates support and participation.

How Bad Communication Can Ruin a Project: Two Case Studies

We've all heard horror stories about the ineffective communication of major change initiatives. I will never forget Dave, a participant in one of my workshops on change management about ten years ago, who described the most recent organizational improvements he was involved in. Dave happened to be one of the union members of a U.S. auto manufacturer. He was selected to serve on a task force to study the implementation of a "quality-of-work-life program" that would benefit all employees as well as the company. The members of the task force analyzed the best programs and the best ways to implement the program throughout the organization. They made a special effort to elicit the support and buy-in of the union as well as the various levels of management.

As soon as senior management approved the task force's recommendation, the change was announced to all employees. Dave was reduced to tears as he described how it was announced by means of a memo sent by management to all employees. The memo offered no explanation and no opportunity for discussion. As a result, it met with complete resistance from employees. He lamented the fact that this had been a wonderful program that had to be scrapped before it ever had a chance to be implemented, all because of poor communication. Seven months of effort completely thrown away. Unfortunately, this scenario is all too familiar.

Although taking *too little time* to prepare an effective communication can result in failure, taking *too much time* to communicate can be equally disastrous. This was the case when a major restructuring was planned at a large manufacturing company. Because of the widespread impact that would result from the change, the plan was to communicate it to all employees by means of small discussion groups led by members who were directly involved with the restructuring.

To reach all ten thousand employees in the organization, the communication took place over a three-month period and had the goal of eliciting buy-in for the proposed restructure. However, during this period, many questions arose regarding the proposal and its implementation, and these questions remained unanswered, producing a growing skepticism among employees.

As a result, the task force reconvened to decide how to answer the questions. Once again, the task force met with each of the employees in discussion groups. By this time, the communication of change was approaching the six-month mark. Now the task force faced even greater cynicism and negativity because employees had discussed the restructuring among themselves for a period of several months, stirring up greater negativity and even more unanswered questions. By the time the task force members completed their discussions, they were forced to abort the restructuring effort that had taken a year to plan and six months to communicate.

It is clear that communication for a change effort has great impact on its success. Too little communication or too much communication can be equally disastrous. The key to effective communication is being clear on your purpose. Many organizations fall into the trap of making "buy-in" their purpose.

Going for Buy-In:
The Trap that Prevents Effective Implementation

For many years, I, too, was an advocate of eliciting buy-in from everyone involved before implementing a change. In fact, buy-in is critical when improvements are made at the employee level regarding the procedures and technical equipment that make up the "tools" employees use to perform their jobs. It makes sense to get buy-in from all employees when decisions are made to improve their equipment or work processes. However, for improvements involving more global issues, such as restructuring, purchasing new computer equipment, or changing processes that impact the organization's culture, eliciting buy-in prior to making the change is less effective and can actually be detrimental to its success.

Indeed, the theory behind eliciting buy-in before moving forward on a project is logical enough. When people agree with a change, they have an easier time supporting and making the change. If, in the process of getting buy-in, employees modify the plan, then implementation will probably be improved on, resulting in less resistance. This makes sense, right? *Wrong!*

When *a mind-set change* is necessary for implementing a new organizational structure, new technology, or new global processes and procedures, then making buy-in the purpose of communication can be a "death trap." What makes a mind-set change different from other changes is that it requires you to view the project from a new perspective. When you are stuck in your old familiar perspective, you won't necessarily see the *value* of the new mind-set. You have to experience it to grasp its value. Even the best sales pitch won't make a difference. As a result, you could easily make modifications to the change to make it less of a "stretch" and compromise its goal of transformation. You can end up spending a huge amount of time soliciting input, only to find that you end up with a "watered-down" version of the change.

What's worse, focusing on achieving buy-in as the primary purpose of your communication of a new mind-set will actually delay the experience of the new mind-set. It is only through experiencing the solutions that we will achieve breakthrough results and prevent the natural resistance associated with adopting the new mind-set. This is one of the great paradoxes of leadership.

The intention to achieve greater support by trying to elicit buy-in prior to implementation often creates even more resistance.

The Impact of Fear on People's Resistance to Change

As the economist John Kenneth Galbraith once said, "Faced with the choice between changing one's mind and proving that there is no need to do so, almost everybody gets busy on the proof."

Most of us are inclined to resist change. Perhaps there's a natural law at work that parallels the law of inertia in physics. In *WordPower*, his dictionary of vital words, preeminent lateral thinker Edward de Bono defines inertia as: "the willingness of things to stay exactly as they are unless moved by sufficient force. We know that this is so in physics and yet we are surprised when it turns out to be the case with organizations."[1]

Communication is the transition from planning (Stage 1) to implementation (Stage 2), both discussed in detail in chapter 10. People react to the planning stage with fear. This is the natural response to being in a situation of "not knowing," which leaves us feeling insecure and out-of-control about our future. It gives rise to worrying, and this encourages our own "what if" scenarios about the future. It is a normal survival behavior to anticipate danger. We respond by thinking about all the possible problems before it happens.

Similar dynamics were in motion when one of my well-intentioned friends warned me, many years ago, about getting into the consulting business. "Most likely you won't be successful," he predicted, "because so many people go out of business in their first five years. However, if you are successful, then you'll probably fail because you'll need to depend on other employees who won't be able to perform to your satisfaction or to the satisfaction of your clients." He was, of course, only "looking out for my best interests" and attempting to protect me from what he saw as certain failure. People who are faced with change also face their fear of the unknown.

It is normal human behavior to avoid fear by running away, procrastinating, or sabotaging the person who is instituting the project or change effort. This is evident in relationships where one person "can't" commit, when we plan to start our diet "tomorrow," or when we avoid starting a

---

1. Edward de Bono, *WordPower*, Penguin, 1990.

project that seems overwhelming. Procrastination and sabotage are the tactics of choice when it comes to avoiding change. When we know that management is holding out for our buy-in before initiating the change, what is the obvious strategy for slowing down or aborting the change? Refuse to buy in!

Sometimes I'm convinced that everyone has read the same manual on how to avoid implementation. The instructions are simple and as follows: "By constantly asking questions about the project, raising doubts about the project, and requesting that managers prove that it will work, you can postpone the implementation indefinitely."

How many times have you seen a project planned and then postponed so that more research can be done, or so that a survey can be conducted? How many times have you seen new task forces created because old ones failed to convince people of the importance of a project?

Ironically, such delaying tactics prove to be far more painful than the process of implementing the project. The anticipation of implementation is almost always worse than the implementation itself because until it begins to take place, people find themselves fighting phantoms.

Involvement vs. Buy-In

Involvement is not the same as buy-in:

- Involvement focuses on *how* the change will be made.

- Buy-in focuses on *whether* the change should be made.

After spending several months assessing the need for a change and planning its implementation, the last thing we need to do is to extend the discussion of *whether or not* we should make the change. Ultimately, there is no right or wrong answer to that question because none of us can predict the future. And when people are nervous about the future, they will most likely choose *comfort* over *risk* and decide, in the end, to keep things the same.

This doesn't mean that you don't need input from affected parties. Input is critical for the decision makers to have a full perspective. But the new direction for the organization is a larger issue that is based on a multitude of external drivers that not everyone in the organization will fully understand because it isn't the nature of their job to see the big picture. Everyone will perceive the proposed outcomes in the context of his or her own particular perspective. There are natural limitations to each person's perspective, regardless of his or her position or level in the organization. Each person's perspective is shaped by the need to attend to the details of his or her own particular job. Most won't be able to see the forest for the trees; nevertheless, their ability to see every knot on every branch of every tree is essential to the smooth, effective operation of the organization.

Similarly, although upper management is in a position to be able to see the full, panoramic view, their ability to see the trees in detail may well be limited. That's precisely why they need input from employees in order to make responsible decisions.

Moreover, most changes involving the future direction of the organization come from *external* rather than *internal* influences. Competition is changing, customers are changing, government regulations are changing, and technology is changing. These are all external drivers that influence the need for the organization to change. But the people working in the organization are focused *internally*. Their perspective is most useful when it comes to translating the new direction into a meaningful operation plan in their individual areas. So naturally we want them involved in implementing the change, but not in deciding the direction of the organization. Because that's not the perspective that they're coming from.

A Place for Buy-In

This is not to say that buy-in isn't desirable. The question is: When is the appropriate time to expect buy-in? When we announce a recommendation at the beginning of implementation, we are presenting our "theory" of the best way to make things better. We don't yet know if our theory will work. How quick are you to accept a theory before you have had a chance to see it in practice? Most of us first want to see proof that the theory works before we buy in to it.

I used to think that the second stage, implementation, was the ideal place for buy-in. Because actions speak louder than words, I assumed that people would buy in to the recommended solutions to implement those proposed solutions. However, when we examine what the common reactions are to each stage of change, we find that the *beginning* of implementation is *not* the best time because people are in a state of chaos and sometimes crisis. It doesn't make sense to expect buy-in when people are experiencing the highest degree of breakdown on their jobs.

Genuine buy-in follows *experience*. How many people believed we were actually going to get a person to walk on the moon before we actually saw it happen on television? Until then, it was a vision that some people believed possible, whereas others did not. The optimal communication time for eliciting buy-in is at Stage 5: Communicating Results of Implementation. Only when people can reflect on their own actual experience with the change can they truly buy in to it.

Communicating the results of the implementation, however, involves more than relaying the successes of the solution. This would be akin to "selling" its success, which, because it is perceived as manipulation, creates more doubt than confidence. People know that no solution is perfect, so it is important to communicate the difficulties and failings of the solution as well as the successes. It is also important to communicate the plans for dealing with those difficulties and failings. Communicating the successes, failings, and plans to improve the failings shows honesty and credibility on the part of management—qualities that are too often lacking in today's organizations.

> Only when people can reflect on their own actual experience with the change can they truly buy in to it.

Most important, management also demonstrates commitment by acknowledging that they are still committed to the solution in spite of its imperfections, and intend to address those drawbacks in order to stay on course. *Commitment* is a vital ingredient. It is unreasonable to expect employees to buy in to the success of the solution or to pretend it's perfect for the organization. Everyone knows this solution won't be perfect and that it will have to be modified to be successful. And they know that in years to come, it will eventually become outdated and be replaced by the next change. Ultimately, employees are buying into management's commitment to the change, and into their commitment to deal with the inevitable problems that will arise. Why should we expect people to invest the effort required to make the solution successful if management is going to throw away its commitment at the first sign of imperfection, only to replace it with the next "flavor-of-the-month" change?

There's another critical reason why Stage 5 is the best time for communication of results: it is at this time that the affected employees will be feeling the most discouraged. This is when employees need to be reassured that, despite problems and failings, the change is, in fact, producing the desired results. Discouragement can be transformed into buy-in and optimism by demonstrating unified commitment and making a clear statement to those people not supporting the solution to either get on board or to find a new train to ride. Buy-in is a critical step in any change process, and it is precisely at Stage 5 when people need their spirits lifted. It acknowledges their accomplishments and renews their commitment to solving the problems that have surfaced.

Communicate to Inspire Action

There are three types of people who can be readily identified in any corporate change effort:

1. There are "active supporters" who like change or believe in management enough to trust that the changes that arise will be better for the organization. They will actively support new solutions no matter what they are.

2. There are "negativists" who are comfortable with the status quo and tend to be chronic devil's advocates or complainers, viewing the glass as half empty even when it's three quarters full. They can be counted on to actively negate and resist the new solution, no matter how well it is communicated.

3. Finally, we meet the "silent skeptics," who have a wait-and-see attitude about the solution. They form the majority, and they don't express any opinion.

Both the active supporters and the negativists openly express their views. They like to be visible, whereas the silent skeptics prefer to stay invisible as long as possible. They are the ones who duck their heads when the facilitator asks for volunteers in a classroom or a team meeting. Let's look at each group individually.

Guess what group usually gets the most attention when we are communicating new solutions? *The negativists.* They, of course, also ask the most challenging questions. We kid ourselves into thinking that if we address all of their concerns and questions, we will be able to convince everyone that the planned solution is going to be successful. However, the negativists aren't trying to win that argument. They don't need to. They can effectively sabotage the success of the solution simply by *raising doubts* in the minds of others. Because no one can predict the future, the negativists create as much doubt as possible in order to arouse fear among the silent skeptics, who are just waiting for an excuse to become negative so that they can remain comfortable as well. The longer we address the negativists' unanswerable questions and concerns, the longer people pick up the negativity, doubt, and fear that goes along with this kind of exchange.

> Guess what group usually gets the most attention when we are communicating new solutions? *The negativists.*

Therefore, the negativists are the last group on which we want to focus our efforts at eliciting support and cooperation for the change. This doesn't mean that we ignore this group. It simply means that we don't give them any more attention in our communication than we give anyone else.

It may appear that the best strategy of communication would be to address the active supporters. Surely, by addressing the supporters of the solution, a positive momentum will be created that will encourage others to participate in the change. However, whereas negativists have great influence on the silent skeptics, active supporters have almost *no* influence. In the minds of the silent skeptics, the active supporters can't be trusted. Why? Because active supporters like everything and can do anything (unlike the rest of us).

The target group for our communication should, in fact, be the silent skeptics. Communicating to this group can be a real challenge, because we don't receive enough input or feedback from them to know where they stand. They rarely express their buy-in for the recommendation because they mainly sit on the fence. However, they are the group that, once involved, can most dramatically influence the success or failure of buy-in.

Stop Selling the Change

The term *buy-in* has always carried with it a notion of *selling*. Otherwise, why call it "buy" in? In the past, we've tried to "sell" the benefits of proposed change instead of just presenting the full story. You might say: "We're going to implement a new solution to solve a problem, and these are all the reasons why you should do it." More sophisticated organizations might even present it in a slightly different manner: "We're going to implement a solution, and to help you understand why, we need to examine the cost of our present situation. Look at all the negatives!"

Both approaches depend on a fundamentally dishonest manipulation of the facts because they don't reveal the whole story. This "sales-oriented" approach creates skepticism, misunderstanding, and confusion about the solution once it is implemented. Often, people go through the motions of the change without really understanding why it is being made. Honest and open communication is at the core of accountability.

There are three keys for communicating to silent skeptics:

1. *Discuss the context for the change.* When you only present the benefits of a change to sell it, the silent skeptics are thinking to themselves, "What aren't you telling me that will cause a problem and that I will be responsible for fixing?" They are sensitive to being manipulated by others. It is important to present the full context for the solution, addressing how it fits into other changes, the recent history of trends in the organization, and its general impact on the organization. Silent skeptics need *understanding* to feel comfortable with the change. They want to understand "the good, the bad, and the ugly" about the change effort. They want to know the "truth."

2. *Show silent skeptics exactly how they fit into the plans.* They want to know as many specifics as possible about the ramifications of the solution on their role, responsibilities, and relationships in the workplace. Their main concern is for their security. This is probably the most challenging part of the communication,

because we can never provide them with as many details as they would like to have in order to feel comfortable. Developing a regular system of communication that updates people on any new information about the change is critical. Otherwise, the "rumor mill" will dictate people's information about the change.

3. *Take action as soon as possible.* The purpose of communicating a change is to create understanding. Although some might not think of taking action as part of the communication, the fact is that some people will not understand a change until they are implementing it. Some people need to experience it first.

When action is taken, silent skeptics who are still sitting on the fence will go with the flow of others in order to avoid being made visible by their resistance. You know that the active supporters will be taking action on the change. So that leaves the negativists, who may be resisting the solution and not taking action. Unlike the silent skeptics, the negativists don't mind showing their resistance and isolating themselves. As long as the active supporters and the silent skeptics are taking action, the change can proceed. It's time we gave our full attention to the people *supporting* the change rather than spending all of our time trying to appease the negativists who are set on resistance.

Once actions are in motion, real results begin to replace the illusions created by the negativists. With proper measurements and tracking, you can demonstrate success fairly quickly and acknowledge the silent skeptics and active supporters for their openness, participation, and contribution to the success of the change. You can also share the measurable results with the negativists to dispel their concerns and, more important, to offer them the opportunity to be part of the successful team. Most will prefer being on a winning team than to stand out as rebels without a cause.

For all these reasons, the sooner the solution is implemented, the better. It is only through action that people can alleviate concerns. The vast majority of fears will vanish when you deal with the realities of the change. When you are taking action, you're too busy focusing on getting the work done successfully to give much thought to whether or not you like the change. You are more likely to think of the change in terms of how you can implement it more effectively. That's healthy, productive thinking that will lead to concrete improvements in the way change is being implemented.

It is fully appropriate to involve people in deciding how best to implement the solution, but not in whether the solution will take place, because that is a given. As problems arise, they will be addressed and dealt with because they are real, not theoretical. This requires, however, that more time be dedicated to evaluation and modification in order to refine the process as it evolves.

You must ask people to suspend judgment while the solution is being implemented. The results will create the buy-in, not in terms of people's opinion, but in terms of a concrete evaluation of how that change has affected the organization's desired outcomes and how effectively it has moved the organization in the clear direction articulated by senior management. In other words, the buy-in will be based on *results* rather than on *theory or opinions* about the impending solution.

Rebels in the Pharmacy: A Case Study

A medical center had been involved with a series of changes for about four years and ran up against a department of rebels (the pharmacy department) that resisted every change. As the organization moved toward patient-centered care, more cross-functional problem-solving teams, and greater accountability, the pharmacy department refused to participate in the change efforts.

Several attempts to remedy this problem by involving the department in training sessions and communication efforts were made, but these efforts did nothing to move the group toward a level of functioning consistent with the rest of the organization. The problem was with the pharmacists themselves. They held the positional and educational power of the department and were unified as a group of negativists that intimidated everyone else, including management.

The organization approached me to discuss the next intervention, which was to bring everyone together to discuss the problem one more time. Hearing this, I thought of the famous definition of insanity, "Doing the same thing over and over expecting a different result." We came up with a new strategy that involved an intervention workshop in which everyone in the department was required to participate. Naturally, many of the pharmacists didn't attend, and those who did either refused to participate or "bad-mouthed" the session. As a result, they were "excused" from attending. This left only the support staff which, although large in number, had previously had no voice in the department due to the influence of the pharmacists.

After the negativists left the session, it didn't take long for participation to increase. The support staff created strategies and agreements for making changes in the department. They developed ways to support each other amid the negativity of the pharmacists. Committed to taking action, they left the session empowered as a team and ready to make changes that they had always wanted to make, but had never had the opportunity to make without having to fear the consequences.

Within a few weeks, other departments were calling the pharmacy congratulating them for the major improvements in customer service, quality, and responsiveness. By the time the pharmacists started complaining about how the changes would never work, the rest of the department had demonstrated a level of success that received public notice. Within four weeks, a four-year-old problem had been resolved, and a new norm of performance and behavior had been established within the pharmacy department.

The case was closed for good, and the pharmacists had the choice of whether or not to stay in the department. Interestingly enough, the most vocal negativists were those who later were to become the most cooperative, whereas some of the more silent ones eventually decided to leave. It isn't uncommon to find a few silent negativists who manage to provoke others to speak out and take the risks of resistance and rebellion.

Six Steps for Communicating Change

Based on our previous section on communication, the following six steps provide a road map for presenting a change effort.

Step 1

Explain the Context for Change

In this step, you are sharing the external drivers that are impacting you which need to be responded to for survival or thriving in the future. These are the "nonnegotiable" pressures that need to be addressed. Also, remind people about the *vision* and *direction* of the organization that this change will contribute to achieving. Finally, you share about the other modifications in the organization that this change will impact. Ultimately, you want people to understand where the change is coming from and what direction it is supporting in terms of the vision of the organization.

Present the Positives and Negatives of the Current Situation

Because you are implementing a change does not mean that the current situation is all negative. People are working hard, and they don't want to believe that their effort is wasteful or not good enough. It is important to list both the positive attributes of the current situation as well as the negative attributes of the current situation, especially in context with the external drivers that need to be responded to and the vision of a better future.

Step 3

Present the Positives and Negatives of the Proposed Change

Rather than *selling* the change, you present all of the aspects of the change. Although you will present the benefits of the change and any positive aspects of the change, you also present the "costs" of the change, including challenges, conflicts, or issues that will need to be addressed.

The strategy here is to be truthful and provide people with a clear comparison between the current situation and the change. The costs of the change represent "pain" for people. These are the issues resulting in fear, obstacles, and setbacks. You want to link the positive and negative attributes of the change and current situation to the external drivers and vision of the organization so that people will make their comparison in context with the *future* rather than the *past*.

There's an old story that if everyone took their troubles outside and placed them on their front lawns in order to have a neighborhood "troubles" exchange, everyone would choose their own troubles. Why? Familiar pain is always more tolerable than confronting an unfamiliar pain that we're not sure we can survive. So even though there may be more pain associated with the current situation than with the proposed situation, many people may still choose the familiar pain over the new pain.

Step 4

Present the Strategy and Action Plan

When you are selling others on the benefits of a change, then your strategy and action plan must focus on ensuring that those benefits are achieved. However, when people are moving into a change effort, their concern is less on the benefits and more on the challenges (reducing the "pain") of the change in which they will need to respond. In this accountable approach to communication, you present the strategy and action plan for minimizing the challenges and costs of making the change.

What are all the ways that the negatives and costs of the change presented in the last step will be addressed? This part of your communication will begin to address people's concerns. It will also let people know that the negatives of the change effort are temporary as compared to the negatives of the current situation which are more permanent (because they have never been addressed). Based on this step, more people will be in a position to give the change a chance.

Step 5

Elicit Involvement

It would be nice if you had solutions to address all of the negatives of the change you are proposing, but this is rarely the case. For the negatives that are still remaining to be addressed, you will create task forces made up of volunteers from the group implementing the change. People will want to get involved in these task forces because they will have a vested interest in reducing any negatives that will impact them. Although you aren't asking people to *buy in* to the change, because it hasn't demonstrated results as of yet, you are asking people to *get involved* with the change effort to ensure success and achieve the organization's vision.

Step 6

Offer the Final Choice

The final step is to give people a clear choice about participating in the change. This is where accountability is established. The importance of providing clear choices is well described by Kathleen Ryan and Daniel Oestreich in their book, *Driving Fear Out of the Workplace*: "Choice increases the positive experience with change. The greater the choice, the better the experience, even when the change leads to hours of hard work, the frustration of ambiguity, and the discipline required to develop new skills or knowledge. When choice is not present, people feel trapped; in extreme cases, they feel like victims."[2]

Although we don't often think this way, there are pros and cons to supporting the change as well as pros and cons to resisting the change. Figure 11-1 illustrates that when you communicate the pros and cons of a situation, you are providing others with the stated consequences for their potential actions. Based on those stated consequences, people can then choose their response. They may or may not *believe* the stated consequences, or they may not *care* about the particular consequences. Based on the choice they make, they will take an action, and based on their action, the real consequences will manifest. Every time the real consequences manifest, it places the person back to a position of choice. Real consequences are based on *truth* rather than what someone *predicts*, so they have more impact on someone's choice. It is also the place that credibility is established between the person stating the consequences and the real consequences.

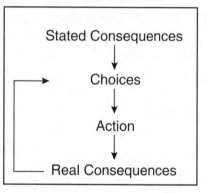

**Figure 11-1:
Informed Choices**

Stated Consequences
↓
Choices
↓
Action
↓
Real Consequences

Applying this concept to my own home situation, I don't allow my eight-year-old daughter to play with a ball near the busy street in front of our house. If she does, I immediately tell her to go inside the house. She can choose to test me and receive the consequence, and then have the opportunity to make a new choice. My goal is to prevent the extreme consequence of her being run over by a car.

In organizations, we are not making people aware of the consequences of their choices. In cases of poor performance, for example, we wait until our customers go elsewhere, which causes us to downsize our organization. By the time we downsize, it's too late for people to make a new choice about their performance; they no longer have a job. The price is high when we lack an accountable work environment, one where expectations and consequences are clearly laid out.

2. Kathleen D. Ryan and Daniel K. Oestreich, *Driving Fear Out of the Workplace*, Jossey-Bass, 1998.

CHAPTER 12

GET STARTED:
YOUR NEXT STEPS
TO ACHIEVE
BREAKTHROUGH RESULTS

MYTH: It takes a year and a lot of resources to create a more accountable organization and achieve breakthrough results.

TRUTH: It takes three to six months to increase accountability and achieve breakthrough measurable results.

A NY LEADER CAN BEGIN TO INCREASE ACCOUNTABILITY within his or her department, with his or her peers, or with his or her direct reports by following the strategy described in the last half of this book. However, for this last chapter, I want to address the larger scale issue of developing an accountable organization.

It is clear that you cannot create an accountable organization through a training program on personal accountability. Although this can help to make everyone aware of being accountable, it won't address the issues of performance execution that involve *teams* of people working together to define accountable practices and habits. It is also clear that you cannot achieve an accountable organization by having managers create *contracts* with each other, because this won't address the issues that arise when someone breaks their contract and doesn't address lower levels in the organization.

It is clear that if you want to develop an accountable organization, you must improve *personal* accountability, *team* accountability, and *cross-functional* accountability. However, what is the best order for accomplishing all of these levels of accountability? What are the key steps necessary to achieve the quickest and most sustainable results? What process can be used to make this a realistic change effort given all of the other priorities the organization needs to accomplish? How do we bring accountability to all levels of the organization in a practical way?

There are six steps to creating organizational accountability, answering all of the questions listed above.

Step 1

Clear Direction from Executives

The critical beginning is to receive a clear direction for change from executives. They must be clear on the vision and business strategy for change based on external drivers, internal goals, and values of the organization. Based on those changes, they must be committed to the development of higher levels of accountability and monitor the efforts and results of being more accountable. They must clearly articulate this direction and provide a picture of the future including the culture to achieve the organization's future state. Their alignment and clarity of purpose are keys for establishing accountability. It simply can't exist without clear intention.

Step 2

Shared Accountability with Middle Management

Middle managers are the change agents for creating an accountable organization. However, they can't do this in isolation where they focus only on their department. They must work together as a team of leaders, directing the organization from an operational standpoint.

In this role, they determine their vision of leadership and their Success Factors of performance execution necessary for leading the organization in a more accountable manner. They take direction from executives and prioritize the operational changes necessary to support the achievement of deliverables taken from the executive team's list of priorities. They develop agreements among themselves for making decisions, sharing resources, and communicating and speaking with one voice to the organization. Breaking down silos, taking ownership for the results of the organization, and establishing more effective habits of performance execution all contribute to the achievement of breakthrough results.

Step 3

Personal Accountability for All Employees

Although middle managers can create a huge impact toward greater accountability and even achieve breakthrough results within a six-month period of time, they cannot sustain it alone. Supervisors and employees at nonmanagement levels must be introduced to accountability and gain clear understanding of the benefits to them and the organization in being accountable.

Using the principles and exercises in *The Power of Personal Accountability*, employees create their own personal vision of excellence along with establishing their personal plan for improvement to become more accountable with their teammates, their customers, and any others they impact in the organization. As each person takes small steps to improve his or her accountability, the entire organization feels the positive impact.

Step 4

Shared Accountability in Departments, Work Units, and Project Teams

As management works more effectively with cross-functional account-ability and nonmanagers are taking more personal accountability, you are ready to achieve even greater breakthrough results, by developing shared accountability in the teams that produce the most results. Department teams, work units, and project teams are the people who serve customers and have the greatest impact on organizational performance. When these teams create a clear vision of excellence, followed by the

---

Success Factors of performance execution that they commit to improving (discussed in chapter 10), performance and morale increases at lighting speed.

It is at this stage that the organization not only exceeds performance expectations, but also develops the core competence of adapting to change. By this time, the organization should have developed benchmark qualities.

Step 5

Accountable Performance Management

Once teams at all levels are operating with shared accountability, management's role is to provide *guidance and coaching* to ensure that every individual is keeping up with his or her agreements and commitments. Managers must have a system for managing performance that enables them to:

- Effectively diagnose the improvement needs for each direct report

- Prioritize the focus of improvement

- Develop effective "nondefensive" forms of communication to coach people

The demand for higher levels of performance increases as organizations become more accountable, and this requires managers to be more watchful of individual performance to ensure that people don't fall behind their team. Accountable performance management provides a dedicated time for managers to acknowledge individuals for their professional growth and contribution to team results and to develop plans for career advancement.

Step 6

Measurement, Celebration, and Renewal

With systems in place for shared accountability with middle management and operational teams, it is important to have a system that tracks measurable improvements in performance execution and the achievement of organizational deliverables that contribute to bottom-line results. Having a system to share these results so the entire organization can benefit from all of its successes is necessary to solidify accountability.

Finally, it is when you are acknowledging success that you can identify areas for improvement and refinement to move your organization to the next level of excellence. This process can last for years, leading to benchmark status and sustaining that position for years to come.

Final Thoughts

Developing an accountable organization is not a fad, or the next flavor-of-the-month change effort. Why? Because organizations require accountability to achieve results. Just as an individual needs to breathe in order to stay alive, organizations need to demonstrate accountability to achieve results. It is the core of employee satisfaction and high performance. Without organizational accountability, an organization cannot adapt to change effectively.

However, there is something else to know about accountability. Whatever problems are solved by being more accountable, you will create new problems in their place. They will be "higher level" problems, and when those are resolved as you become more accountable, you will have new even "higher level" problems to resolve. The good news is that as you develop higher levels of accountability, you will be able to solve all of those problems and more—resulting in greater strength and much greater success.

Your task is to get started—to take action. Your task is share this message with those around you in order to build the momentum and support to create greater levels of accountability—and with it higher job satisfaction, higher levels of performance, and greater success than you ever thought possible.

INDEX

Are You Ready to Increase Your Personal Success and Satisfaction?

The Power of Personal Accountability

This practical book provides a road map for translating your dreams and desires into clear intentions. You will learn a practical approach for changing habits that undermine your success. You will learn the secret to being accountable—developing "recovery plans" to prevent the trap of "perfection" that causes discouragement. You will be able to identify when you fall into the "victim loop" and learn practical steps for getting back on track to achieve your goals. You will feel inspired, clear, and ready to take action.

"Sophie and Mark have produced a terrific operations manual for getting and staying in the driver's seat of your life. It's an ever-valuable reminder that no matter where we find ourselves, in a moment's notice, we can get positively engaged in where we want to go."

From DAVID ALLEN, Author,
Getting Things Done: The Art of Stress-Free Productivity

. . . .

*For more information, visit us at www.impaqcorp.com
or call us at 800 332 2251.*

Are You Ready to Deepen Your Skills and Assist Your Organization?

Two Workshops

The Workshop—Creating the Accountable Organization

Now that you have completed the book are you ready to take your next step?

During this one-day highly interactive workshop, you will review the primary principles discussed in *Creating the Accountable Organization* and practice several tools and techniques described in the book. You will also learn several additional techniques not described in the book to enhance your leadership abilities.

Workshop Outcomes

- Assess your organization's level of accountability
- Review and apply the Accountable Process for Change
- Develop your Personal Vision of Leadership
- Identify a new Habit of Performance Execution (Success Factor)
- Learn how to facilitate Success Factors and Measurements for improvement
- Apply an Accountability Based Questioning Technique to coach others
- Learn a strategy for overcoming the "Wall of Fear"
- Establish action plans for increasing accountability

The Workshop—The Power of Personal Accountability

Take the ideas and strategies taught in the book and put them into immediate action through the one-day workshop, The Power of Personal Accountability. You will become clear on your intentions and assess your strengths and areas for improvement. Based on this assessment, you will develop a clear strategy for taking action to increase your effectiveness, communication, and ability to hold others accountable who impact your life. You will develop questioning skills, recovery plans, and a support system that will help you take action to achieve results.

Workshop Outcomes

- Assess your personal areas for improvement
- Identify a strategy for coaching yourself and others
- Learn how to overcome mistakes quickly and turn those into opportunities
- Get yourself and others through resistance to change using specific tools
- Become skilled at holding others accountable and dealing with negativists in a supportive manner
- Discover an action planning system that includes "proactive recovery" to ensure success
- Develop a process for acknowledging and recognizing success

. . . .

For more information, visit us at www.impaqcorp.com or call us at 800 332 2251.